Jossey-Bass Teacher

Jossey-Bass Teacher provides educators with practical knowledge and tools to create a positive and lifelong impact on student learning. We offer classroom-tested and research-based teaching resources for a variety of grade levels and subject areas. Whether you are an aspiring, new, or veteran teacher, we want to help you make every teaching day your best.

From ready-to-use classroom activities to the latest teaching framework, our value-packed books provide insightful, practical, and comprehensive materials on the topics that matter most to K–12 teachers. We hope to become your trusted source for the best ideas from the most experienced and respected experts in the field.

"How do you expect me to learn anything when you're the one who keeps asking all the questions?"

The Science Quest

Using Inquiry/Discovery to Enhance Student Learning, Grades 7–12

Frank X. Sutman • Joseph S. Schmuckler • Joyce D. Woodfield

JOSSEY-BASS
A Wiley Imprint
www.josseybass.com

Published by Jossey-Bass

A Wiley Imprint

989 Market Street, San Francisco, CA 94103-1741—www.josseybass.com

Readers should be aware that Internet Websites offered as citations and/or sources for further information may have changed or disappeared between the time this was written and when it is read.

Limit of Liability/Disclaimer of Warranty: While the publisher and author have used their best efforts in preparing this book, they make no representations or warranties with respect to the accuracy or completeness of the contents of this book and specifically disclaim any implied warranties of merchantability or fitness for a particular purpose. No warranty may be created or extended by sales representatives or written sales materials. The advice and strategies contained herein may not be suitable for your situation. You should consult with a professional where appropriate. Neither the publisher nor author shall be liable for any loss of profit or any other commercial damages, including but not limited to special, incidental, consequential, or other damages.

Jossey-Bass books and products are available through most bookstores. To contact Jossey-Bass directly call our Customer Care Department within the U.S. at 800-956-7739, outside the U.S. at 317-572-3986, or fax 317-572-4002.

Jossey-Bass also publishes its books in a variety of electronic formats. Some content that appears in print may not be available in electronic books.

Library of Congress Cataloging-in-Publication Data

Sutman, Frank X., (date)
  The science quest : using inquiry/discovery to enhcnace student learning, grades 7–
12 / Frank X. Sutman, Joseph S. Schmuckler, and Joyce D. Woodfield.
        p. cm.
  Includes bibliographical references and index.
  ISBN 978-0-7879-8586-8 (pbk.)
  1. Science—Study and teaching (Middle school) 2. Science—Study and teaching
(High school) 3. Inquiry-based learning. I. Schmuckler, Joseph S., (date) II.
Woodfield, Joyce D., (date) III. title.
  Q181.S88 2008
  507.1'2—dc22
                                                              2007044563

Printed in the United States of America

FIRST EDITION

PB Printing   10 9 8 7 6 5 4 3 2 1

Contents

*We dedicate this book to all of the teachers of science who strive
to improve the future for their students and for the nation.
We also dedicate it to our families, who offered us constant support,
and to Lorraine Corbett and Janice Lathrop, who helped to put
the manuscript into readable and manageable form.*

Preface

Eureka! That word alone brings to mind the excitement of true scientific investigation, of the inquiry and discovery process that is fundamental to the development of the world as we know it today. The goal of this book is to help teachers find ways to carry that excitement into their own classrooms.

The Science Quest is designed for practicing and preservice teachers who are searching for a more effective approach to science instruction, and especially for a better understanding of how to implement "inquiry"-oriented practices in classrooms, grades 6 through 12. The book explores in detail an approach we refer to as "student inquiry/discovery" and offers a practical framework for supporting students both in developing critical scientific thinking skills and in gaining standards-based content knowledge. Science supervisors, science teacher educators, and even college-level science instructors should also find this book of interest. Teachers of mathematics and language arts who are sensitive to the need to integrate basic skills and science can benefit from this book as well.

In the present school environment, we too often as teachers have overheard a student say, "I hate science. It's so booooorrrrrrrring." Although science should not be presented as the latest "infotainment," we do need to consider how conventional lecture-and-test instruction (or "cookbook" lab routines) can leave students indifferent. Science as a process of inquiry, research, exploration, and overall discovery is anything but boring. From ancient times, seekers of knowledge have explored the visible world and struggled with the data they collected, finding ways to forge it into the body of knowledge that we call science. For example, England's Royal Academy of Science sent forth expeditions in search of new species, invited the public to join them in meetings to welcome back those explorers, listened enthralled to the explorers' descriptions, publicized the results of their findings, and debated their significance. Today, whether taking televised journeys deep into space with NASA or deep into the ocean on ventures exploring marine life, the public remains enthralled with the outcomes of scientific inquiry and discovery. And we all live more comfortably and take for granted the huge body of knowledge that is the physical evidence of these successful quests for knowledge and understanding.

Today we look at the somewhat dismal results of standardized testing in science, as in other fields, and listen to critics who decry how our students stack up against other countries in science performance and wonder, What has gone wrong? The premise of this book is that we as a nation have lost sight of the quest. We have developed a science instructional approach that provides answers that do not provoke questions, especially effective science questions, and that do not develop seekers of knowledge. Too often students do not seek—they are given questions to answer. Students need to be taught how to ask the right questions, to seek the answers, and to critically evaluate their findings on the basis of how well these "fit" what is already known. More specifically, students need to gain skills and experience in scientific inquiry, reasoning, and practice, especially if they are to be prepared for continued study of science at the college level. It is the purpose of this book to support teachers in making that happen in their classrooms.

Inquiry and discovery are hallmarks of the scientific enterprise. Supporting and building on the recommendations of the National Research Council in its two important publications, *Inquiry and the National Science Education Standards: A Guide for Teaching and Learning,* (2000) and *Taking Science to School: Learning and Teaching Science in Grades K–8* (2007), our book offers an innovative method for enlivening science lessons and improving learning outcomes through the inquiry/discovery instructional framework. The approach emphasizes two major processes: (1) engaging students in scientific "inquiry" questions, and (2) enabling students to "discover" answers to their questions through participation in hands-on investigative experiences and related activities. Students gain valuable experience in scientific practices (observing, collecting data, analyzing results, drawing conclusions) while also building their skills in mathematics and language. Inquiry/discovery instruction places high importance on the teaching of language through classroom discussion, research reading, and report writing. Although students find such experiences more challenging, they also find them more interesting and enjoyable.

Students begin the inquiry/discovery process by becoming engaged in relatively simple activities, taking on greater investigative responsibilities as they gain in skill and proficiency. The process can be successfully introduced to fifth-grade students, but provides for sufficient levels of rigor to challenge advanced-placement high school students (or even college-level students). The book provides detailed guidance on how to build inquiry/discovery practices into conventional science lessons and laboratory routines and includes numerous case descriptions of sample lessons along with useful lesson planning and assessment tools. The sample lessons have been developed by the authors and have all been tested in real-world classrooms. For the purpose of demonstrating our approach, the lessons include content of limited complexity but are designed to show how the instructional process can work in multiple science disciplines and with students at varied levels of preparation and readiness. Though all of the lessons feature hands-on investigative activities, all use relatively simple materials, some of which can be gathered or constructed by students themselves; none require elaborate laboratory facilities or equipment.

It should be mentioned that the purpose of inquiry/discovery instruction is not to supplant the teaching of content. By encouraging an experiential understanding of scientific concepts, it serves to deepen understanding, making the content more memorable and meaningful to students. Teachers under pressure to cover a curriculum emphasizing "breadth over depth" may also have concerns about finding the time to engage in inquiry/discovery instruction, which often takes longer to implement than conventional approaches. However, it should be noted that inquiry/discovery activities do not need to be incorporated into each and every science lesson or laboratory experiment for students to benefit. Instead, these experiences can be built into lessons selectively, and are ideally suited for introducing important new science ideas and conceptual understandings. Eventually, over the course of a year, students will gain increasing skill and proficiency for carrying out these activities on their own, requiring less instructional oversight and planning time.

The inquiry/discovery approach was developed by the Center for Science Laboratory Studies (CSLS) at Temple University, through funding from the National Science Foundation and other public and private agencies, and is supported by over a decade of case study research conducted by the authors, both in training science teachers and in observing science instructional practices in a variety of school settings. The approach is being used by numerous science teachers who have participated in preservice and professional development programs conducted through CSLS and its related arm, the Multicultural Education Resource Information and Training Center (MERIT Center). These teachers have found it to be effective and rewarding for their students, benefiting low achievers and high performers alike. And as we explain in Chapter Three, research also shows that the approach appeals to English language learners (ELLs) and has enabled them to perform better on standardized science and language tests in comparison with their peers. Although not confirmed by formal studies, numerous anecdotal reports suggest that inquiry/discovery practices have served to inspire students to pursue advanced studies in science at the college level.

For those of us who teach in the sciences, considerable challenges lie ahead. In May of 2006, the National Assessment of Educational Progress (NAEP) released the 2005 "Nation's Report Card" (Grigg, 2006). The summary of this report indicated that "science understanding by students at grades 4 and 8 remained flat compared to previous years. And the performance of students at the 12th grade level is especially disquieting, with the average science test scores dropping slightly."

Hardly a month passes without another urgent appeal from either the scientific community or the broader business community and governmental agencies across the nation to improve our approach to science instruction in ways that will better prepare students to contribute to and survive in the new global economy, and especially to enable students to become more effectively prepared and increasingly enthused about science and about entering science-related professions. The appeals do not end there. Efforts to increase the level of scientific literacy across the nation, thus enhancing public understanding of and support for the scientific enterprise, are called for as well. The way we teach science has a great impact on the science that is learned and on whether or not our students become sufficiently interested in the subject to pursue the advanced training required for entering scientific professions.

The Science Quest offers everything a teacher needs to begin effective inquiry/discovery instruction. In Chapter One we explain what is meant by "student inquiry/discovery" and what it looks like in practice as we profile two very different approaches to a middle school science lesson. In Chapter Two we describe typical activity sequences in an inquiry/discovery lesson, including approaches for addressing the standards as well as how best to involve students before, during, and following hands-on investigations. In Chapter Three we present a series of lessons showing how inquiry/discovery learning experiences can be introduced in stages by starting students with simple activities and enabling them to take on increased levels of challenge as they gain in skill and proficiency. Chapter Four includes sample lessons for the middle school level. Chapter Five features high school–level lessons. In Chapter Six we focus on the importance of language for developing students' critical thinking and inquiry skills. We also provide suggestions on working with students in teams and with students who have special needs. Chapter Seven provides guidance on student assessment, including tools for assessing skill learning, content understanding, and readiness to take on inquiry/discovery tasks. Chapter Eight provides suggestions for managing the inquiry/discovery classroom and for obtaining necessary laboratory resources. In Chapter Nine we offer parting thoughts and advice. In short, this book will serve as a guide and friend throughout your career, as you take responsibility for preparing the next generation of scientists and scientifically informed citizens.

Frank X. Sutman
Joseph S. Schmuckler
Joyce D. Woodfield

About the Authors

Frank X. Sutman, Ed.D., first experienced inquiry/discovery science instruction as a college freshman, under the guidance of faculty who were scientists and who were dedicated to preparing teachers of science for the school level. He successfully practiced this instructional approach during his early years of teaching science at the middle and high school levels and continued the practice later when, after completing his doctoral studies at Teachers College, Columbia University, he entered college-level teaching of science content and science pedagogy. Sutman has held faculty positions with several institutions over the years, including William Paterson University, Interamerican University of Puerto Rico (where he initiated the certification program in science and mathematics teaching), and State University of New York at Buffalo. His longest association was with Temple University, where he served twenty-six years as professor in the division of Science Education, including as chairman of the division, and also directed two major centers affiliated with the division: the Center for Science Laboratory Studies (CSLS) and the Multicultural/lingual Education Resource Information and Training Center (MERIT Center). These centers supported school-level science teachers in conducting doctoral-level research related to inquiry/discovery science instruction and also to become prepared to teach multicultural/lingual school-age students. It was through these centers that much of the case study research related to the instructional approach depicted in *The Science Quest* was conducted.

Sutman has held numerous visiting positions in science teacher education nationally and abroad in China, India, and Israel. He was also invited to serve for four years as visiting program director in the Education and Human Resources Directorate at the National Science Foundation, where he had responsibility for overseeing curriculum development projects, grades 5–12, and for assessment of student learning in science projects.

Sutman has published numerous professional monographs and journal articles as well as three science textbooks that he coauthored. These are now part of a collection at the Chemical Heritage Foundation in Philadelphia. In addition, he has served as president of both the Association for Teacher Educators in Science (ATES) and the National Association for Research in Science Teaching (NARST), as a Fellow of the American Association for the Advancement of Science (AAAS), and as a member of Sigma Xi (the scientific research society). He is recipient of several awards, including the Albert Einstein Award granted by the governor of New Jersey for outstanding teaching and service to minority students and their teachers. Currently, Sutman serves as consultant and adviser to science teacher education programs, most recently at Richard Stockton College, where he teaches and serves as mentor and supervisor of science teacher interns.

Joseph S. Schmuckler, Ed.D., first experienced the inquiry/discovery emphasis in the teaching of science as a graduate student at the University of Pennsylvania. He taught school-level life sciences and chemistry for many years, during which he also served as associate researcher at the Sun Oil Company and Sadtler Research Laboratories. He was a member of the writing team for the National Science Foundation's (NSF) supported curriculum, Chemistry in the Community (ChemCom), which is a laboratory-driven middle and high school–level instructional program that merges chemical theory with its applications. He contributed to *Chemical Achievers*, published by the Chemical Heritage Foundation. This program details the roles of minorities and women throughout the scientific enterprise. Schmuckler also served as an adviser to the development of the video presentation *100 Most Important Science Discoveries* for the Discovery Channel as well as to the *NOVA* TV series in "The Life of Percy Julian."

He taught chemistry to nonscience majors and to teachers of science during his over-thirty years as professor of science education at Temple University. He also taught courses related to the teaching of science for pre- and in-service teachers, including "The Scientific Industry" and "The History of Science." All of these courses emphasize the significant role that the laboratory contributes to the scientific enterprise. He also continues to serve as a mentor and supervisor to science teaching interns and as an adviser to teachers of science pursuing certification and master's and doctoral degree studies.

Schmuckler has been recognized for outstanding science teaching through receipt of the following awards: The Philadelphia Chamber of Commerce Award, the Pennsylvania Department of Public Instruction Award, the Manufacturing Chemists Benjamin Rush Award, the James B. Conant Award for High School Teaching of Chemistry, the Christian

Lindbach Award of Temple University, and the George Washington Carver Award for Outstanding Teaching of Minority Students.

He has been an invited visiting professor of science/science education at Tianjih Namal and Shanghai Universities in the Peoples' Republic of China and has given workshops throughout China and in several European countries over a period of fifteen years.

Joyce D. Woodfield has been teaching English language and visual arts, including photography and computer graphics, for both middle and high school–level students for more than thirty years in the Baltimore County Public School System. She has participated in conducting professional development workshops for teachers, called "Writing Across the Curriculum" and "Assessment of Learning Strategies," with a focus on developing alternative hands-on means of assessment such as gallery worksheets and self-assessment tools. She is a member of the Johns Hopkins Chapter of Phi Delta Kappa and was an active long-term participant in the Teacher Researchers Institute of the Baltimore County Public Schools, under the direction of Marcie Emberger. Mentored by her husband, Charles W. Woodfield, former teacher and science supervisor for the Baltimore County School System, she has spent years in Benjamin Bloom's "Blooming World of Action Verbs." She both thinks and talks in Bloom with its educational emphasis on academic rigor, and educational emphasis and enjoys applying Bloom's thinking frameworks to language and writing instruction related to science-based content.

The Contributors

Dr. Alexandra B. Hilosky   professor of science, Harcum College, Bryn Mawr, Pennsylvania, and adjunct professor of chemistry, Temple University, Ambler Campus

Dr. Anthony S. Lombardo   science teacher and former assessment and data analyst, Rosetree/Media School District, Pennsylvania

Dr. Holly D. Priestley   science teacher, Burlington Township High School, Burlington, New Jersey, and adjunct science education instructor, Pennsylvania State University

Dr. William J. Priestley   science teacher, Harry S. Truman High School, Levittown, Pennsylvania, and adjunct science education instructor, Holy Family College, Philadelphia, Pennsylvania

Dr. William R. Smith   science teacher and department chairman, Bristol Township High School, Bristol Township, Pennsylvania, and school coordinator, NSF Funded Curriculum Project, Villanova University

The Science Quest

Chapter 1

Rethinking How Science Is Taught

WHAT SHOULD BE OUR GOAL in the teaching of science? Lynn Margulis, a world-renowned microbiologist who is the former president of Sigma Xi (a highly respected organization of research scientists), wrote the following in her "President's Message" column in the November-December 2005 issue of *American Scientist* (a journal of Sigma Xi): "Francis Bacon, who some consider to be the father of modern western science, wrote over 350 years ago, 'for what a man more likes to be true he more readily believes.'" She stated in her column that, "We scientific researchers resist this natural tendency. We do not try (only) to be true. We discount gossip. We disdain common myth. We seek hard evidence. And when doing science, we try to avoid the influence of faith-based dogma. *Yet all of us who participate in science share one common faith. We believe that the material energetic world is knowable, in large part, through the concerted activity of research, exploration, reconnaissance, observation, logic and detailed study that includes careful measurement against standards* (italics added)."

Margulis goes on to state that, "supposedly we are the richest and freest country in the world. Then why do 15 year old U.S. students rank 22nd of 40 countries in science literacy, according to the latest survey conducted by the Organization of Economic Cooperation and Development (OECD)?" She concludes that "this condition may result (for the most part) from a contradiction in our national psyche, a deep cultural divide in that truths are (too) often sacrificed to what most people like to be true and thus more readily believe."

Critical Thinking and Inquiry

The messages of Francis Bacon and Lynn Margulis have particular relevance to us as science teachers and as authors of this book. That is because we have a special responsibility to set as one of our teaching goals

1

the preparation of ourselves and our students to overcome the "natural" tendency to believe as fact that which we like and to discard that which we do not like even though it has been proven. We as teachers of science overcome this tendency first by inquiring about our own understandings and then by expecting our students to do more than listen and memorize factual information. Rather, it is our responsibility, through schooling, to prepare (even train) students to inquire into their own understandings and thus to become educated to think in the way that scientists do. Although it is important for students to understand the content of science, it is equally essential that they learn about the purpose and methods of science (this can be called the "scientific enterprise"). This means that we must expect our students to develop habits of mind and critical reasoning skills that enable them to participate effectively in the scientific process: to grapple with scientific problems, to question conventional wisdom, and to be able to seek out hard evidence in support of their arguments. A recipient of the Nobel Prize in physics, Sir William Henry Bragg, stated it this way: "The important thing in science is not so much to obtain new facts as to discover new ways of thinking about them."

In the past decade, numerous publications have called for "inquiry" approaches to science instruction that can effectively help students develop critical reasoning capacities, including the ability of students to pose scientific questions and investigate them, to accurately record and interpret the results, and to be able to link their findings to a developing body of scientific knowledge. The most significant of these publications is *Inquiry and the National Science Education Standards: A Guide for Teaching and Learning* (National Research Council, 2000). This document provides detailed standards along with guidelines for introducing inquiry as both an experiential process and the goal to be met through K–12 science instruction. (The specific standards for grades 6–12 learning will be addressed in later chapters.) In a more recent report, *Taking Science to School: Learning and Teaching Science in Grades K–8* (National Research Council, 2007), the National Research Council (NRC) continues its emphasis on science instruction that directly engages students in the *practice* of science, citing the following four proficiencies to be developed for all students in grades K–8:

1. To know, use, and interpret scientific explanations of the natural world.

2. To be able to generate and evaluate scientific evidence.

3. To understand the nature and development of scientific knowledge.

4. To participate productively in scientific practices and discourse.

The NRC report indicates that "these strands of proficiencies in addition to representing learning goals for students as well, need to serve as a broad framework for curriculum design."

Understanding Student Inquiry/Discovery

Although much has been written on the topic of inquiry, understanding it, especially as it applies to instruction, has proven to be challenging to many science teachers. This is because the term has been used with different meanings when applied to education. The NRC, in *Inquiry and the National Science Education Standards*, has its own definition, and in addition, many states have their own particular definitions as expressed in their science education standards. We will take up the specific NRC "inquiry standards" a bit later in this book, but here's a basic description for *inquiry* included in the Standards document as applied to instruction: "When engaging in inquiry, students describe objects and events, ask questions, construct explanations, judge these explanations against current scientific knowledge and communicate their ideas to others."

The instructional framework proposed throughout this book is based on a simplified and clearer understanding of inquiry, especially in reference to the role of students. Most English-language dictionaries associate *inquiry* with the verb "to inquire," which is defined in *Webster's Collegiate Dictionary* as "To ask about, to put to question or to seek information by questioning." This definition has naturally led some to the conclusion that inquiry simply is the single skill of asking questions. In instruction, the important distinction is that the inquiry process can be either student-directed or teacher-directed. A major goal of our instructional process should be to encourage students to take the initiative in posing the questions or inquiries.

You have probably noted that young children begin to inquire using the word *why* ("Why is the sky blue?" for example). Parents attempt to answer such questions, not always successfully. Nevertheless, children continue to ask these kinds of questions often well into the early grades. In the later grades, however, students become less inquisitive and, as teachers too often have observed, rarely ask questions except those that relate to instructional procedures or to the grades they have received. Instead they appear to sit and absorb knowledge like little sponges, until tested, when they reveal they have absorbed very little, unlike sponges. A major reason for this is that they have become "tuned in" to the idea that it is a major role of teachers to ask them questions. Therefore, they have "tuned out" any queries they might have to areas of confusion, being satisfied (at least on the surface) with "covering" the material under study.

In the inquiry/discovery approach, teachers are encouraged to restructure their presentations to reduce lecturing and asking their students questions and instead, to open the door for students to do the inquiring, with the teacher providing guidance and encouragement, at least until students return to what was once a natural and useful habit. Eventually, with such guidance, students will inquire profusely, even asking questions that are of higher order: questions that, for example, begin with words such as *how, which,* and *why* (the inferential), rather than simply *who, what, when,* and *where* (the observable). Inquiry-oriented instruction enables students to practice and develop the particular skill of asking higher-order questions that are relevant to the area under study.

We now turn to an understanding of *discovery* related to its use in instruction. According to the *American Heritage Dictionary, discovery* is defined as "the act or instance of discovering or of something discovered through those actions." Notice that the term is used as both a verb (a word of action) and as a noun (a label for the results of the action). We follow this dual usage as well when we state discovery is the investigative process that students undertake in response to inquiries (preferably their own inquiries), including the findings and outcomes of that process. Unlike student inquiry, which involves only one skill (effective questioning), the process of student discovery involves the development of many investigative skills. In science, for example, the critical skills include observing, reasoning, measuring, mathematical manipulation of data, preparation of tables and graphs, and interpretation of data, all used in the processes of explaining and developing valid conclusions. Other skills, too often not historically associated with science instruction, that are not emphasized include the following: virtually all language skills (reading, writing, speaking); wondering; explaining; editing; revising; discussing; thinking; and analyzing. Thus we conclude that inquiry and discovery-oriented instruction enables students to develop and practice many investigative skills in the search for answers to their own inquiries. Students, in effect, become researchers. Of course, as students pass from one grade to the next, the necessary resources that they seek in the practice of discovering must be attainable or students will, once again, stop inquiring and discovering.

Although student inquiry and student discovery are distinctly different, as we have just described them, they are in fact closely intertwined. Many professional educators have referred to the combination of the two simply as "inquiry." We prefer the term *student inquiry/discovery*, because it helps to remind us, as teachers, to increase the involvement of our students in both processes symbiotically. Therefore we continue to emphasize the combined terms throughout this book.

Teaching Strategies for Inquiry/Discovery Learning

In his foreword to the NRC Standards book (2000) mentioned earlier, Bruce Alberts, president emeritus of the National Academy of Science, refers to *inquiry* as a "state of mind." Although it is true that inquiry requires new ways of thinking, developing these habits of mind, especially through hands-on experiences, is not yet standard practice in many science classrooms. In part, this is because teachers lack guidance in designing investigations in ways that facilitate students' practicing and learning to inquire and think critically about evidence and then to discover. Our goal in this book is to show how the inquiry/discovery process not only enlivens lessons based on or driven by laboratory investigations, but also builds deeper understandings of science content. This instructional approach offers a framework for structuring lessons so that students can and will become more deeply engaged and take greater interest in their learning.

Before introducing our lesson-planning framework in Chapter Two, we here portray two different ways of teaching a science lesson: (A) a didactic or teacher-centered approach, and (B) an inquiry/discovery-oriented approach. Both lessons focus on the concept of "force and motion" for the middle school level.

Lesson A: Force and Motion (Conventional Approach)

Student Learning Objectives:

- To correctly define the terms *force, motion, speed, velocity, acceleration,* and *inertia*

- To be able to solve mathematical problems that involve these terms and thus to understand their meanings and how they relate to one another

We enter the classroom of a middle school teacher of science, where the teacher is asking students to review the definitions of the terms *force, motion, speed, velocity, acceleration,* and *inertia,* which he had presented on the previous day. When students are asked to give examples, several refer to the assigned reading from the night before. Some students are unable to answer the question, having not read or understood the assignment. The teacher uses that opportunity to introduce the objective and procedures for today's lesson. Students open their textbooks, and individuals answer questions posed by the teacher from the reading. The teacher then uses the book material to introduce the mathematical formulas pertaining to force and motion, as well as velocity and acceleration. He then demonstrates on the chalkboard the use of a "plug-in" technique for calculating answers to those problems, based on the set formula. Meanwhile, the students watch him and copy the solutions. The teacher then assigns the students to use the same procedures to solve the next four problems at the end of the chapter. He moves around the room as they work, checking their procedures. For homework, students are asked to complete the remainder of the textbook problems independently. The students are given the timetable for completing the unit: a review the next day, a test on the problems the following day, and a final review of the material when the teacher returns the tests the following week. The plan for this sequence of lessons is as follows:

Lesson Plan (Force and Motion):

- The teacher will describe and define the terms *force, motion, speed, velocity, acceleration,* and *inertia.*

- Students will read the chapter, and the next day the teacher will introduce it by asking them to answer questions about content from it.

- Before the end of the period, the teacher will solve four sample mathematical problems related to force and motion: numbers 1 through 4 at the end of the chapter (day 1).

- Students will solve problems 5 through 12 at the end of the chapter for homework, and the teacher will review these during the next period (day 2).

- A test on definitions and solving plug-in problems will be given (day 3).

- Eight days later, the teacher will review problems that were solved incorrectly on the test and will correct definitions, orally.

Comments on Lesson A (Conventional Approach)

According to the lesson plan, most of the instructional activity is the responsibility of the teacher. The students are only given responsibility to read the chapter "Force and Motion" and to solve mathematical problems, and be prepared to answer questions asked by the teacher about the content. The activity consists of having individual students respond orally to the teacher's questions about the material "covered" and then follow the teacher's directions in completing the problems. Experience indicates that students do not usually respond well, if at all, to such teacher-generated questions, for several reasons: students have not read the assignment, they have read the assignment but do not understand it, or the teacher does not offer each student called on enough time to think about and respond effectively to the questions asked. Very often the teacher ends up answering each question him- or herself. Teachers often attribute this poor student response to the students' unwillingness or inability to read the text. Either way, students often are unable to effectively interpret the meaning of the content. Rather than addressing the causative factors that produce this outcome by modifying their instructional strategy, teachers continue to repeat the unsuccessful instructional approach over and over, especially in providing both the questions and the answers. This particular approach to learning encourages students to be "nonparticipants" in their own education. The result is apathy to the assignment and, ultimately, to the subject matter itself. This form of instruction, often referred to as the traditional or didactic approach, not only places an increased instructional burden on teachers, it also leads to lower morale for both teachers and students, resulting in a lowered efficiency of learning. It is truly teacher-centered and, as indicated, it is very ineffective in enhancing students' understanding of scientific content and in developing their interest in science as a field of study.

Lesson B: Force and Motion (Inquiry/Discovery Approach)

We approach the classroom of another middle school science teacher, Miss Biggs, teaching the same material. To convey the classroom dynamics, the lesson is presented in a narrative form. The student learning objectives are briefly noted below, but as you will note, the objectives are not revealed to the students until the lesson evolves.

Student Learning Objectives:

- To understand the meaning of force and motion, and how the terms *speed*, *velocity*, and *acceleration* are related to these

- To learn how to solve mathematical problems associated with force and motion and how the mathematics formulas correlate

- To develop skills in posing questions, preparing graphs, analyzing data, and summarizing content knowledge

This sixth-grade teacher begins this sequence of lessons on force and motion by indicating to her students that for the next few days they will be exploring the characteristics of a moving wagon and the distance it can travel, over time (four seconds). This period of time enables an investigation to be carried out safely in a school hallway. The teacher's instructions to the students are as follows: "First, let's look at the materials we will use. They include a wagon with the bolt at the base of the handle tightened so that the wagon will only be able to move in a straight line. In addition, we will use a long strip of wrapping paper about eight meters in length, a meter stick (with both English and metric units), masking tape, Magic Markers, scissors, bathroom-type scales, several physical science textbooks,

FIGURE 1.1

Investigating Force and Motion.

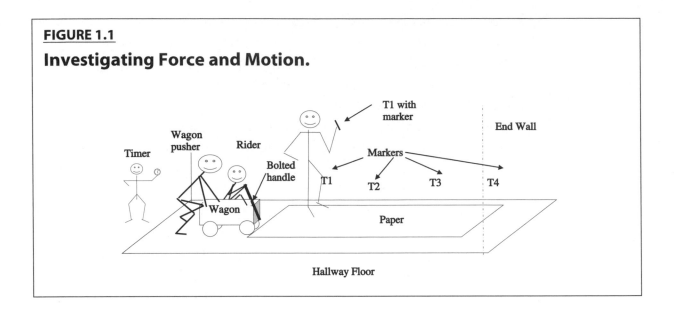

and historical references." The teacher points out that all of these items will be important tools for students to use as science investigators.

She divides the class of thirty students into seven teams of about four each, with each team including students of varied levels of proficiency. Each member of each group is eventually assigned to carry out one of the activities that make up the investigation. Each student is given a copy of the printed directions for carrying out the procedure that includes a diagram (Figure 1.1). One student from each group is called on to read the procedure out loud to the rest of his or her group. Each group is invited to ask the teacher any questions about the procedure. Only two questions are asked: "Who will ride in the wagon?" and "Who will push the wagon?" The answer is automatic; two students volunteer, accompanied by considerable laughter and joviality.

The class gathers in the hallway, which serves as the "informal" science laboratory. One student notices that the hall is carpeted, unlike the classroom, where the wagon would move more easily. She asks if that is important. The teacher responds first by congratulating the student on her excellent observation. She then asks the student to write the question on the chalkboard when the class returns to the classroom and further comments that, once the initial investigation is completed, the class will return to this question and other questions during a follow-up investigation.

Two students from Group A are assigned to follow the directions indicated by the diagram (Figure 1.1) and to tape the wrapping paper along the hallway floor. To ensure safety, the teacher makes certain they provide enough distance between the far end of the paper strip and the end of the hallway to allow the wagon to complete its approximately four-second journey without crashing into the wall. Another two members from Group A align the front wheels of the wagon along the outside edge of the paper strip. With great fanfare, the two volunteers, one to ride, the other to push, take their positions. First there is a trial run. A student from Group B volunteers to be the starter and practices counting, "3, 2, 1, go!" A second student from this group volunteers to be the timer. Using a stopwatch, she practices counting each second, "1-1,000, 2-1,000, and so on" that the wagon moves. (No stopwatch is actually required, because counting "1-1,000, 2-1,000, and so on" is a consistent measure of time.) Students in Group C squat in various positions along the side of the paper strip nearest to the wall, and with Magic Markers in hand, mark the point where the front wheels of the wagon are in line on the paper strip at the end of each second counted.

Following the trial run, the student who volunteered to ride in the wagon is weighed, and this is recorded for future reference. Then the investigation officially starts. As soon as the wagon begins moving, the Group C students mark on the paper the distance traveled each second for the total of four seconds. Group D students use the markers to consecutively number each section of the paper strip and then cut across the strip at each mark, producing four segments total. Following the cutting, each segment is measured and its length recorded on the strip, marking the distance the wagon traveled during each second of time.

Returning to the classroom, Group E students mount the segments of paper consecutively onto the wall, with the bottom edges resting horizontally on the floor (Figure 1.2). The teacher then calls on Group F students to describe, verbally, what the length of each strip of paper represents and to indicate why the directions called for placing the strips next to each other in this way. With the teacher's support, the students eventually recognize that the paper strips provide visual representation or a "bar graph" of the wagon on its journey. They are asked to label the horizontal and vertical axes of this incomplete graph. The students then discuss the length of each segment, noting with some controversy that some segments were measured in metric units (centimeters) and others in English units (inches). The teacher encourages them to consult a handbook that is available in order to convert all the measurements to one system of measurement.

For the final activity of the instructional period, the teacher invites the students to observe the bar graph and to draw it in their notebooks as a record of the collected data. She then asks students to think about what they have observed and to develop within each group questions that need to be answered and points that need clarification. In formulating their questions, the teacher requests that the students include at least four questions

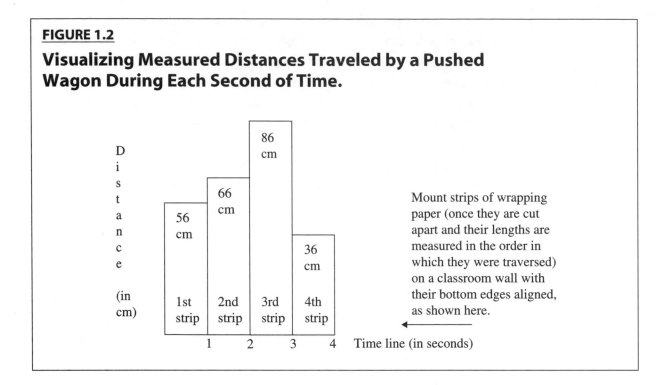

FIGURE 1.2

Visualizing Measured Distances Traveled by a Pushed Wagon During Each Second of Time.

that involve numbers. The example given was, How far did the wagon travel during the four seconds? They also were to include certain terms (*inertia, force, motion, speed, velocity,* and *acceleration*) in their questions. She encourages the students to consult the textbook chapter on force and motion or other available references to help them clarify each definition. At the end of the period, the questions developed by the student teams were presented to the class and then consolidated and sequenced for follow-up discussion the next day. Some of the questions raised by the student teams were

- Why did the wagon move farther during some seconds than during others?
- What caused the wagon to speed up? To stop moving?
- Where does the energy come from to cause the wagon to move?
- Would the data be the same if there was no friction between the wagon wheels and the floor? Suppose the floor had not been carpeted? Suppose there was a heavier (or lighter) student in the wagon?
- What if the wagon had been allowed to roll down a hill? What if it were pushed up a hill? How would this data look on a graph?
- How far did the wagon travel or move during the first three seconds?
- How much slower did the wagon travel during the fourth second compared to the third second? Why?

- What was the average speed (or is it velocity) of the wagon over the four seconds? How do speed and velocity differ?

- How much farther did the wagon travel during the second second than during the first second?

The teacher then reviewed the day's activity with the students, reminding them that they were to be prepared the next day to answer the questions that they generated. The teacher pointed out or reminded them that some of their answers must be mathematical, and that the students should carefully think about the relationships among the terms used in the questions, referring as necessary to the textbook chapter.

The next day the teacher invited students to present their answers and explanations regarding the questions posed the previous day. She also discussed the use of mathematical formulas as a means of finding answers using data collected by others. The teacher concluded the session by informing students that the "test" related to this investigation will be a letter that each student writes to a friend, explaining what the class did, the conclusions they have come to, and what they had learned. She reminded them that like any good narrative, the letter needs to include clear statements of events as they occurred as well as explanations of what was learned throughout this activity. Also, the test will call on each student to design three mathematical problems related to the data they collected and to solve each problem correctly. Each student also is to design a parallel problem using a car or an airplane in place of the wagon. All problems are to be solved and the answers clearly stated. Following is an example of a letter written by one of the students to a friend in which she describes the activity and the results that were obtained.

October 2, 2008

Dear Jose,

In our science class over the last few days, our teacher, Ms. Biggs, had us conduct an experiment in which we analyzed what happened when a wagon was pushed down the hall, outside of our classroom. This was fun because we saw Bill ride in the wagon. Everyone wanted to have a turn. We measured how far the wagon moved each second over four seconds, after Mary used enough force to overcome the wagon's inertia. We placed a paper strip on the hallway floor and marked on it where the moving wagon was at the end of each second. Then we measured these distances and marked the measured distances on the paper strips and cut the strips.

Then we went back into our classroom and taped the strips on a wall to make a bar graph. Our teacher asked us to write questions about the moving wagon that involved the data we collected. Here are examples of questions that I wrote:

- How far did the wagon move during the first two seconds?

- How much farther did it move during the second second than during the first second?

- What was the average speed of the wagon over the four seconds?

- What percentage of the total distance did the wagon move during each second?

- How accurate were our measurements?

To answer our questions we looked up in our science book the meanings of words like force, motion, inertia, friction, speed, acceleration. Our teacher helped us to use these words in studying the graph. Oh, I almost forgot to say that one team measured the distance the wagon moved in feet while the other three groups used centimeters. This meant that we had to find out how to convert all of the distances to the same unit of measure.

This was a fun lesson. We gave the graph a title: "The Moving Little Red Wagon!" Our teacher told us that we would have an opportunity to apply what we learned to other examples such as a moving car. I'm working on this problem now. Hope your science classes are as much fun and you learn as much as we do!

Sincerely,
Mary Ellen

Comments on Lesson B (Inquiry/Discovery Approach)

The letter indicates that the students' involvement made the science learning more palatable than if the content had been presented using the usual didactic approach. In addition, students gained experience in applying mathematics skills to science and in searching for information rather than simply listening to the teacher present the information. Of course, learning does not fully develop from a single experience like that described in the preceding case history. However, the approach results in students wanting to learn more. Perhaps even more significant is that the instructional approach emphasized here results in students becoming engaged in a hands-on investigative experience; the approach will also encourage students to pose their own questions, to experience gathering evidence (data), and to gain experience in discovering or developing conclusions. There are many additional aspects of science teaching that are addressed more extensively throughout this book.

As we shall see in the next chapter, it is possible to obtain significant improvement in students' scientific thinking skills through a better understanding of the true nature of "reformed" instruction. Thus you can be assured that by emphasizing certain teaching strategies and procedures in instruction, as described in later chapters, not only will you be able to address the objectives and goals that are so crucial to the nation's future well being, but most immediately important, your students will gradually meet these objectives and goals.

Chapter 2

Linking Inquiry/Discovery and Content Learning

THE NATIONAL SCIENCE EDUCATION STANDARDS (National Research Council, 2000) interchangeably refer to *inquiry*, *the nature of science*, *the scientific method*, and even *science* itself as having somewhat similar meanings. Although it is encouraging to find that *inquiry* is primary to an understanding of science, it is important to keep in mind what the standards call for: having students learn science content and become familiar enough with the nature of science that they can understand and emulate it.

The "content" of science refers to its many disciplines (and subdisciplines), such as biology, chemistry, physics, geology, anthropology, and so on, each of which is concerned with a specific body of knowledge and includes the theories and conceptual ideas that cross all of the disciplines. Inquiry, as we now know, is the first step in the process used by scientists to uncover that which they seek to understand and, as a term, simply refers to asking relevant higher-order questions. Discovery is both the process of gaining scientific knowledge and skills and the culmination of what is learned. Combining the learning of content with inquiry/discovery practices is what we call "the scientific enterprise." Enabling students to understand the nature of this "enterprise" is a major goal of the inquiry/discovery instructional approach.

With that in mind, we move into the crux of this book. How do you create lessons that, from their inception, actively engage students in the mastery of science content? The key is to move students closer to being the source of the knowledge, not just the recipient. Unless students are actively engaged in identifying this content and the methods of pursuing this content, they will remain, at best, passengers rather than engineers on the trip. How do we put them in charge of investigations without us as teachers abandoning control of the process?

15

The Importance of Hands-On Activities

Although inquiry can play a role in instruction across the academic disciplines, the inquiry/discovery process is most effectively introduced and taught in classrooms when teachers call upon materials that students use to carry out investigative activities that lead to the collection of information (data). The process of collecting, observing, and summarizing information, especially numerical data, is effective in stimulating lesson discussions and for developing the desired critical thinking skills. Students need to experience scientific conclusions based on precise observations and collected data, and that these conclusions can have greater accuracy and validity than those based on other types of evidence. For the purpose of explaining our instructional approach, the lessons described in this book start with relatively simple hands-on experiences requiring minimal (and inexpensive) supplies, moving to more complex investigations. All the lessons, however, involve students in the critical evaluation of data, and often require elementary mathematical computations as well as the creation of graphs and other numerical representations.

Lesson Planning Considerations

When planning lessons that are to generate student inquiry/discovery, teachers need to remember what most intrigues people. Students are new to many things we have often forgotten to be surprised and excited by. Perhaps stretching back to those questions asked by the very young would offer inspiration for developing lessons. Why is the sky blue? And when it isn't, why is it those other colors we see? Why does the Moon look so much bigger when it is closer to the horizon?

Works such as the Website Wikipedia, which defines or explains many subjects, or James Burke's *Connections* TV series (Burke, 1979), in which he identified the investigative links among science discoveries over centuries (the water wheel to clocks, to the Jacquard loom, to the modern computer, for example) can be of great assistance to the science teacher. Sharing with students some of those "puzzles" and sequences and providing the names of Websites offering other conundrums for examination might well elicit enough student-asked questions on any topic to generate a year's worth of lessons, while staying well within the guidelines set by local and state education departments.

In designing activities with a goal of encouraging student inquiry/discovery, the following assumptions are essential:

1. Student inquiries also generate student answers on discoveries.

2. Students are significantly involved in investigations from the outset.

3. The teacher avoids personally or directly answering most student inquiries.

4. The teacher directs students to varied discovery resources for answers or conclusions related to students' inquiries.

To enable these assumptions to prove successful, the scope of lessons must be finite, with reasonably immediate outcomes that generate and encourage further discovery activities; that is, further experimentation to challenge the primary premises of the students' understandings of science. Thus the sources for content do not only come from curricular expectations, they also originate from the personal experiences of students and teachers and from the students' interests as they probe for relevance in response to readings and to direct observations.

Teacher-Student Roles in Investigations

A fundamental role of science teachers should be to present an investigation to the class. Traditionally the teacher states the parameters within which the investigation will proceed (with specific focus, precautions, and background information). The teacher gathers supplies, materials, sources of information, and diagrams of the assembly process, especially if students are to create their own equipment. She or he then supervises setup procedures and oversees the investigation itself, being particularly mindful of safety procedures, the goals of the ongoing investigation, and the collection of inquiries raised by students as they work.

This practice does not change in inquiry/discovery classrooms. However, students are given significantly more opportunities for involvement and initiative as the investigations are carried out. Rather than answering student questions as they arise, the teacher either stops the presentation to have the students address these questions themselves or may accumulate student inquiries for further discussion and responses with the class, as a whole, at the end of the activity. In the process, the teacher encourages the inquirers to discuss their questions with classmates and to formulate possible responses or to create additional inquiries that direct them to answers from references that must be readily available to them. Thus the teacher guides students to sources for discoveries and for drawing conclusions (including those that go beyond the scope of the investigation itself).

The teacher may revert to the more traditional instructional approach by providing the format for organizing and analyzing responses, or, better, he or she may lead students to develop their own format, depending on the level of the subject being taught and by assessing students' earlier understandings and their readiness to undertake more independent activities. Here the mode may also differ, depending on the degree to which student inquiries play a role in understanding the outcome of a given investigation.

Inquiry/Discovery Lesson Activity Sequence

There are three essential phases in an inquiry/discovery lesson: Pre-Laboratory, Laboratory, and Post-Laboratory. These phases in turn may be broken into five separate segments or steps, each of which might take place during a different instructional period. To summarize, the lesson sequence is as follows:

Pre-Laboratory Phase

1. *Inquiry:* Problem or topic is proposed for study.

2. *Method:* Investigative procedure is planned.

Laboratory Phase

3. *Investigation:* Activity or experiment is carried out.

   - Evidence or data are collected or observed.

   - Data or results are analyzed.

Post-Laboratory Phase

4. *Conclusions:* Answers or explanations are summarized.

5. *Extension:* Applications are discussed and related inquiries are explored or investigated.

The preceding sequence of activities roughly corresponds to the scientific process itself. In some ways this sequence compares to the introduction, lesson, and summary of the conventional lesson. However, there are significant differences, beginning with the way the teacher approaches the lesson (generating student interest and questions), then with the follow through (the apportioning of student responsibility for both the progress of the lesson and its outcomes) and how the summary is handled (open-ended, geared toward the idea that the topic is an ongoing area of study).

The degree to which the teacher involves the students at each of these stages depends on several factors: the teacher's own comfort zone, the students' and teacher's prior experience in this area, and the students' abilities to adapt to exploration and questioning as a fundamental part of their education. As we will discuss in Chapter Three, the process of introducing and developing student inquiry/discovery within the science classroom is gradual, not instantaneous, and can take place in months, even over the course of a year.

Establishing Learning Goals

Instructional planning for inquiry/discovery investigations should be approached with particular student learning goals in mind. These usually include objectives for both content learning and inquiry/discovery skill development. As we saw with the wagon investigation in the previous chapter, however, it may not be necessary or appropriate to reveal the learning objectives to the students at the outset. Instead, essential knowledge related to the lesson was left to the students themselves to discover. In resolving their own questions about the data, students had to begin to understand not just new concepts (for example, force, motion, inertia) but also a rationale for knowing them. Thus understanding the goals or outcomes became self-evident to the students.

Content Standards

Effective science teachers continue to keep sight of their responsibility to make curricular links with expectations set for teaching. Their overview has to remain clearly in place, and they must remain ready to answer this question, for themselves: "What is the minimum that my students are expected to know, and when?" Each teacher can, for example, create a grade-level checklist in cooperation with colleagues, especially with those who teach at the next grade level, to evaluate the degree to which students will address and meet, for example, the criteria set by the National Research Council's (NRC's) "Inquiry Instructional Standards" and perhaps as well as by the "benchmarks" included in the *Atlas of Science Literacy* (American Association for the Advancement of Science, 2001, 2007), and state and local testing parameters.

In addition, there needs to be, at appropriate intervals, a "reality check." "Where are we now? How does this activity tie in with previous investigations, areas of student curiosity, or current affairs as they relate to what we are doing to form natural links among activities? Where can we expect to go from here?" This reality check is necessary if a coherent whole for students is to be achieved.

Diagnostic Probing

Student assessment has special importance in the student inquiry/discovery-centered curriculum and will be addressed in some detail later in the chapter. Diagnostic (preactivity) assessment of concept attainment is especially significant here, because it establishes the framework upon which further learning rests, both in terms of content and developed or underdeveloped process skills. The specific focus of this probing should be, What do we need to learn now? or What have we not learned? That is, What weaknesses have previous activities revealed, especially in areas of student confusion (mass versus weight, chemical equilibrium, or biological versus other forms of evolution as examples)?

The conventional strategy for assessing understanding is for teachers to ask of students the generic question, "Are there any questions?" This approach usually elicits no response, or unhelpful responses such as "I guess not." Another approach, one that demands students' responses that can quickly be assimilated by the teacher, is "probing." The teacher supplies students with color-coded cards that they hold up when the teacher asks, "Have you understood this concept?" (A green card indicates yes, a red card indicates no.) This form of response produces far superior results than does obtaining few or no responses with the earlier described approach. When a high percentage of red cards are showing, the teacher then knows to readdress the concept. A high percentage of green cards indicate it is time to move on. In each case, it might be helpful to pair students (red with green) to spend a few minutes "comparing notes" or understandings, resulting in the generation of statements of confusion to be addressed (a variation on the familiar pair-and-share activity). Although on the surface this appears to be time consuming (and that clock keeps ticking away), it is important to remember that we teach students, not the subject. If they don't understand the groundwork that has been laid, they certainly will not understand what we attempt to build on top of it.

Important to the purpose of the science classroom is establishing students' familiarity with appropriate and safe laboratory procedures to be followed. The necessity for diagnostic assessment in areas of procedures cannot be underestimated. For example, the safe and correct use of the pipette is vital, especially in handling corrosive solutions and in biotechnology investigations.

Inquiry Standards

As stated already, the learning goals should also include development of inquiry/discovery skills. The fundamental abilities to be emphasized at the middle school and high school levels have been detailed in the National Research Council's Standards document (2000) and are listed here.

Content Standards for Science as Inquiry

For Grades 5–8

- Identify questions that can be answered through scientific investigations.

- Design and conduct a scientific investigation.

- Use appropriate tools and techniques to gather, analyze, and interpret data.

- Develop descriptions, explanations, predictions, and models, using evidence.

- Think critically and logically to make the relationships between evidence and explanations.

- Recognize and analyze alternative explanations and predictions.

- Communicate scientific procedures and explanations.

- Use mathematics in all aspects of scientific inquiry.

For Grades 9–12

- Identify questions and concepts that guide scientific investigations.

- Design and conduct scientific investigations.

- Use technology and mathematics to improve investigations and communications.

- Formulate and revise scientific explanations and models using logic and evidence.

- Recognize and analyze alternative explanations and models.

- Communicate and defend a scientific argument.

Necessary Classroom Tools and Resources

There are forms of support that, if considered in planning for instruction, will facilitate student inquiry/discovery. A given is that science teachers need to have available the kinds of equipment and supplies that when used by students, lead to exciting and challenging experiences for both students and teachers. Beyond this, the science classroom must look different from classrooms in which other subjects are taught because student inquiry/discovery doesn't just occur in laboratory settings or just during follow-up discussions. The classroom setting needs constantly to remind students that a significant purpose of science education is to prepare them to inquire and discover. Following are essential features that should be included.

The Laboratory

The major resources for use in student inquiry/discovery-oriented science instruction, of course, are the formal and informal laboratory settings. Here is where students inquire and discover answers to their inquiries through handling or manipulating traditional and nontraditional scientific equipment and materials. This equipment and these materials need not always be extremely technical, nor should they be. Furthermore, the rapidly increasing development of computers, calculators, CDs, Websites, and so on makes it possible for students to substitute technological simulations for certain hands-on experiences that perhaps have been considered important, historically. Additional considerations about laboratory practices will be discussed later in the book in reference to specific lessons.

Bulletin and Query Boards

A "bulletin board" should be centrally located for posting science-related articles, quotes, illustrations, and student-developed reports. Students should be encouraged to consult the board during discussions and while carrying out laboratory investigations. The "query board" serves as a location for the teacher to post significant inquiries asked by the students themselves. These materials are posted on both boards, usually with only minimal comments ("teasers" to further excite student curiosity).

A box of "credit slips" may be provided as well, on which students are encouraged to record relevant questions to be answered about different topics that are introduced. When filled out, these slips are stapled to the query board for others to consider, next to the items that generate or generated the inquiries. Credit slips are also used to record "answers" or investigation tips found by students in responses to inquiries generated during current ongoing investigations. Thus students receive credit for participating in all aspects of each board's development. In fact, any student or teacher may add appropriate materials related to instruction to either board.

Discovery Resources

An even more important feature of the inquiry/discovery classroom, however, is the "resource center," where basic science references, journals, and other print materials, including items from the Internet, are available to encourage further independent discoveries. A single textbook should not be considered effective as the source of all information. Students should be encouraged, even expected, to consult these resources at various phases of their investigations, especially in summarizing evidence or in assessing the applications of their findings. Teachers may wish to grant students additional credit for assisting in collecting and updating these adjunct resources, including the updating of Website information. Many hundreds of resources, both in print and online, are available to teachers for supplementing textbook readings. A list of selected resources is included at the end of this book as Appendix A.

A Sample Lesson: Study of Archimedes' Principle

Now that the classroom supports are in place, let's observe two classroom activities that demonstrate how inquiry/discovery can be incorporated into a lesson unit: Exploring Archimedes' Principle. The unit starts with a teacher demonstration of displacement effects on water levels followed by a hands-on student activity in which students investigate sinking solids. The learning goals of the first activity (a teacher demonstration) are specified in the example, although this is not initially revealed to the students. Archimedes' Principle itself is not introduced to students until later in the lesson.

Activity A (Floating-Sinking Boat Demonstration)

Student Learning Objectives:

- To develop the understanding that two "matters" cannot occupy the same space at the same time

- To develop an understanding of displacement, in reference to floating and sinking objects

- To begin to develop observation and questioning skills as well as an understanding of the difference between guessing and hypothesizing

The teacher fills a large rectangular plastic container (a fish tank, as an example) with enough water so that when a smaller second container or "boat" is pushed down into the water, the water will not spill over the top edge of the larger container. Then the teacher places the "boat" into the water and pushes down, holding it so that the level of the water just reaches the top edge or rim of the "boat" (Figure 2.1).

The teacher then challenges his students to describe any change that will occur in the depth of the water when he sinks the "boat." Most of the students predict that the water level will rise. Some predict that it will not change. To generate even greater understanding, the teacher has students vote on what the results will be!

Many of the students are surprised to note that the water level drops as the boat sinks! Following this observation, their teacher points out that decisions or predictions made by scientists are based on direct observations, not on the results of voting. Then he requests that each student write at least one inquiry that comes to mind during observation of this unexpected result. Most students write, "I expected the water level to rise, why didn't it?" Others write, "Why didn't the water level stay the same?" Responding to these inquiries is delayed until the following demonstration is completed.

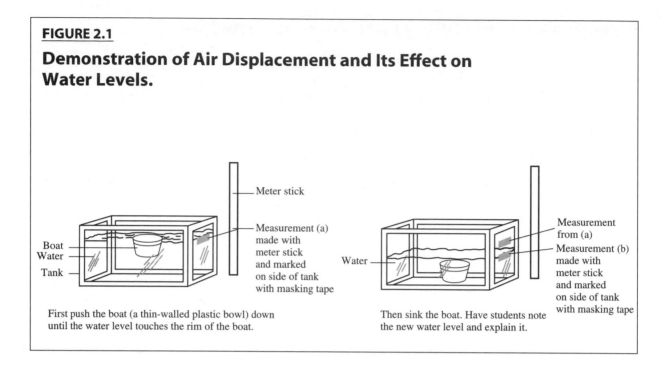

FIGURE 2.1

Demonstration of Air Displacement and Its Effect on Water Levels.

Meter stick

Measurement (a) made with meter stick and marked on side of tank with masking tape

Boat
Water
Tank

First push the boat (a thin-walled plastic bowl) down until the water level touches the rim of the boat.

Water

Measurement from (a)
Measurement (b) made with meter stick and marked on side of tank with masking tape

Then sink the boat. Have students note the new water level and explain it.

Now the teacher turns the boat completely upside down so that the air is trapped inside. Then, after asking the students to describe what he has just done, he pushes the "boat" into the water until it is completely submerged, upside down. The students observe that the water level rises. Then the teacher tips the "boat" so that the students can observe the once trapped air escaping through the water. Students now note what happens to the water level as the air escapes.

Comments on Activity A

These two related simple demonstrations offered students an opportunity first to predict based on inadequate information and then an opportunity to explain why many of them initially drew the incorrect conclusion. Continuing the opportunity to observe further, the students discovered that in the first trial, the water displaced the volume of air inside the boat, causing the water level to drop. They learned that simply voting led to an incorrect explanation and conclusion. They initially had inadequate information for making an accurate prediction. Demonstrations or investigations that lead to unexpected results can motivate students to explore further, even to pose further inquiries such as, "Do scientists ever vote in drawing conclusions? Is voting an effective way to resolve an investigative question?" Eventually students learn that a goal of science is to be able to explain that which is observed and to do so with accuracy based on adequate observations and knowledge.

FIGURE 2.2

Follow-Up Investigation: Sinking Solids.

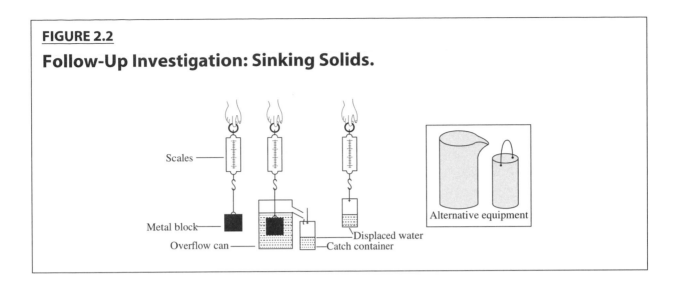

Scales

Metal block

Overflow can

Displaced water

Catch container

Alternative equipment

Activity B (Sinking Solids Investigation)

Involving students in this follow-up investigation carries their conceptual understanding of sinking objects to another level. The learning goals and the student and teacher roles are described in the lesson sequence. Before proceeding, the class is divided into student teams, with each group given the following materials and instructions, along with the "sinking solids" setup diagram (Figure 2.2).

Materials: An overflow can, a metal block (that fits inside the overflow can) with an attached thin hook or wire, a graduated cylinder, a spring scale, string, a metric ruler, a catch bucket, and water.

Students also have the following written instructions:

Student Instructions

1. Measure and calculate the volume of the metal cube in cm^3 (units) and its mass in g (units).

2. Place water in the overflow can up to its spout.

3. Tie the wire to the metal cube and carefully suspend the tied cube totally in the water, allowing the displaced water to flow into the catch bucket. Measure the volume of the displaced water and determine its mass.

4. Determine the mass of the cube again while it is immersed in the water.

5. You now have the following data: volume of the cube, mass of the cube (in air and its mass when it is suspended in water), volume of the displaced water, and mass or weight of water displaced by the cube.

6. Compare the following collected data:

   • Volume of cube and volume of displaced water.

   • Mass of displaced water. (Mass and weight are numerically equal.)

- Mass of cube in air and its mass when suspended in water. From this data calculate the difference in mass of the cube in the air and when it is suspended in water. Compare any difference to the mass of the displaced water.

7. Draw conclusions from your collected data, and include these conclusions in a written summary report of the investigation. These conclusions, as part of the report, should be written by each student.

Post-Laboratory Phase: Through participation in the investigation just described and follow-up discussion, and by consulting references, the students learn that a solid displaces a volume of liquid equal to its own volume. And they develop a conclusion, stating, "The apparent loss in weight or mass of the solid, when suspended in water, is equal to the weight of the displaced water." The teacher follows up the report of the investigation by asking students to develop inquiries from these experiences and to include their inquiries and responses to them as an appendage to their final written report. With some direction from the teacher, students pursue answers to these questions: How does mass differ from weight? How are they alike?

In the course of these related investigations, students pose a number of inquiries, among them, "Why didn't the water level rise when the boat was pushed into the water?" "How do we know that the volume of displaced air is equal to the volume of the boat?" "Why does change in the weight of a solid occur when it is placed in a liquid like water?" "How can we explain the different results obtained by different groups of students?" "Does the weight of an object in air equal its weight in a vacuum?" "Why is what we observed called Archimedes' Principle?" "What are some practical applications of displacement?" These questions are recorded and placed on the query board. They become the basis for extended searches and considerable discussion.

During the extension stage of the investigation, students in groups are encouraged to explore Archimedes' Principle further and are directed to print and online resources, including Google, which has links to extensive historical references, applications, and further explanations. Students are also referred to the book *How Things Work*, authored by John Langone (1999) and the article "Reading Between the Lines" (2007), which describes an early document written by Archimedes nearly 2,500 years ago. Group members present their summary findings to their group, and each group then prepares a written summary report to be posted on the query board.

When the teacher finds that many of the students are excited by the entire series of investigations, he encourages them, as a further extension activity, to determine whether thin sheets of metal that are denser than water can be made to float. (The students accomplished this by curling up the edges of thin metal sheets of aluminum foil, to form "metal boats.") This leads other students to, for example, inquire, "Does determining the weight of an object in air give you an absolute result or only an apparent weight?" These students are sent to the Web to explore "air's impact on weight." Still other students, observing the aluminum foil investigations, are invited to investigate, on the Web, how submarines submerge.

Comments on Activities A and B (Archimedes Lesson)

The common practice of beginning a lesson or lesson sequence by asking students, "What do you think will happen?" and then making certain that they know what will happen, or what the outcomes should be, defeats the intent of the inquiry/discovery approach. The "what do you think …?" approach also leads to ineffective scientific thinking processes because no incorrect response to this form of questioning can be given! Another reason for not using this questioning approach is that students do not have the opportunity to learn how to understand or differentiate between guessing and hypothesizing. The approach simply brings closure to the opportunity to practice inquiry and thus to related discovery, of which hypothesizing is a part.

Too often teacher demonstrations of how science "works" tend to stifle questions rather than generate them. In Activity A, for example, the demonstration itself raised questions and was effective in introducing hands-on activities that were built upon the earlier experiences, both of which demanded that students inquire about what they had seen and what they did. In part, this occurred because the first activity was a "new" experience, so students were made aware that their preconceptions may be faulty (a valuable lesson in scientific reasoning). It was also the result of the teacher's refraining from telling students in advance what they would experience and why it "works" the way that it does.

To have facilitated learning even further, the teacher could have assigned each student to record, in writing, at least two inquiries that emanated from the demonstration, and included this same assignment in the follow-up investigation. These inquiries then would have served as the basis for further searching and discussion.

Instruction Supporting Inquiry/Discovery Lessons

Fortunately today, science teachers have available to them an expanded scope of activities, including those provided as simulations, with information available from the Internet and a wealth of articles and current events to support their lessons. There can be so much to do that teachers may have to remind themselves to intersperse activities with opportunities for student questions and discussions related to a given topic. Discussion is an essential component of practice in inquiry/discovery learning. In guiding such classroom discussion, it is the teachers' role to keep students focused on the topic that is being studied.

An effective approach to instigating discussion is the presentation of *team summaries* of investigations by a spokesperson for each student team. Such summaries are valuable in that they invite questions that lead to further discussion of investigative outcomes and for exploring the implications of the topic being studied. Teacher-generated questions, "thrown out" at opportune moments, can also lead to discussion and brainstorming. For example, "So, how can what we have learned be applied in real life?" The idea conveyed by this teacher-asked question is that student science investigations are not merely a replication of known information but also can become the bridge to new ideas and possibilities: the stuff of careers to come.

Inviting Student Questions

Teachers who are aware that their science students rarely, if ever, inquire beyond, "How do we do …?" may themselves ask, "How can I cause my students to begin to meaningfully inquire beyond the procedural?" As seen in the Archimedes lesson, inquiries begin to flow when students are presented with question-provoking activities that demand further investigating, not just physically, but also mentally. When the participants piece together what they have observed with what they already know, identify what they don't know, and find new avenues of inquiry, they bridge the gap between what is already known and what is yet to be learned.

An effective instructional strategy is for teachers to ask students fewer questions during instruction, especially questions that can be responded to merely by students recalling short bits of factual information or with no response. The recall type of interaction deters students from thinking, as well as learning to inquire, at higher and more significant levels. That is, such short, abrupt (recall type) interactions between student and teacher lead to closure rather than expansion in thinking. Once a short answer is forthcoming, there is nothing more to consider or to discuss.

Organizing the Class into Teams

Teamwork is considered essential to the development of student inquiry/ discovery during instruction, and it's often advisable that the class be grouped into teams before a lesson begins. When students function alone, they are less likely to raise questions. Even if they are puzzled by an occurrence, they tend to disregard the event in favor of getting the task done. If a solution occurs to the lone student, it is often too briefly noted. In contrast, pairs or teams are not linear in their approach. They diverge, investigate tangential information, circle around, and continue to challenge and to prod for answers. To facilitate interaction, teams should be held accountable for their time and productivity. Use of the "Research Team Feedback Form" (Exhibit 2.1) can serve as a means of causing student teams to develop efficient and effective coordination to better meet the expectations set by the teacher. This form can also be used for reporting and for assessment purposes. Those uses are addressed in more detail later in this chapter and throughout the book.

Selecting and Working with Teams

An important preparatory step to teamwork concerns team organization. This includes selection of team members to integrate strengths and weaknesses of members (either mix or match). Other factors include optimum team sizes—usually three to four members. (With fewer members there can be problems completing expected work efficiently. With greater numbers, some members become idle, allowing a few to do the work for all.) Then there is tasking (finding ways to break down activities into specific aspect), with each team member assigned a function within the team. Timing is important; assume group task assignments will take less time than it would for one or two students to complete what has to be accomplished; plan minimal times that are realistic (time should and can be added as needed). The prospect of having "too much" time encourages students to be dilettantes rather than diligent. Even consider using a timer to encourage productivity.

It is important that student teams complement each other or work together. The process of "jig sawing" is often effective for generating individual participation in group activities. This and other approaches for working in teams are addressed in Chapter Six. Groups themselves need to recognize that the segments of investigations that they undertake "interlock" with activities for which the entire class is eventually responsible. This interlocking process stimulates each team to perform because it can't just "borrow" the results from another team. Knowing or sensing that their work or contribution is to be sequentially coordinated with that of other teams (that they are not all replicating the same events) generates excitement and curiosity about each group's part of the whole. It also encourages alternative views and approaches. At times, of course, the

EXHIBIT 2.1

Research Team Feedback Form.

Date: _____   Each Group Member's Name _____ initials _____

_____ initials _____

_____ initials _____

Table Number: _____   _____ initials _____

Procedure: This form serves to develop a record of each research team's participation in scientific investigation. Simply follow the headings to produce a complete record. Each team completes one form and returns it to the teacher.

- General title of the topic being investigated: _____
- Specific focus of your team: _____
- Identify the assignment of each team member. Also state the information or discovery gained as well as its source (by investigation in the laboratory, through reading, or through another source). Be specific.

_____.

_____.

_____.

_____.

_____.

Initials:

- Write a summary of the procedure and discovery(ies) obtained *by each team member.*

_____

_____

_____

_____

_____

Initials:

- List one or two additional inquiries developed by your research team that still need to be pursued. Indicate the team member accepting responsibility for those inquiries with initials.

_____

_____

_____

_____

Initials:

opposite approach brings greater meaning to an investigation, when the closeness of results across groups supports reliability and perhaps validity. The teacher needs to develop sensitivity to the appropriateness of each approach to group activity. Students, of course, need to become aware that both organizational approaches to investigating are typically practiced by scientists.

Assessment in Inquiry/Discovery Lessons

Assessment, too, is essential to inquiry/discovery learning and takes place before, during, and after investigations. Assessment is based on a variety of measures, such as oral and written queries posed by students during investigative procedures, group reports and individual student investigative reports, traditional content tests and quizzes, and the teacher's informal observations of how well students participate in lesson activities. (Assessment practices will be covered in greater detail in Chapter Seven.) The most important tool to be mentioned here is the Research Team Feedback Form.

Research Team Feedback Form

As indicated earlier, student groups should be judged in terms of the time they spend on a study area and their overall performance. A practical means for the teacher to gather evidence for evaluation when multiple groups are functioning simultaneously is to use a form like the Research Team Feedback Form (see Exhibit 2.1). This form provides every member of a student-research team a place to identify him- or herself, to state the specific contribution he or she made, and to initial when he or she has completed the contribution to the overall inquiry/discovery process. This form calls for students to consider among themselves, with initial teacher support, the major inquiry to be investigated by the team and the specific focus (for the group) of the investigation. If the team is responsible for a specific component of the class's overall investigation, the form allows for feedback concerning the nature of that component. This form also includes space to record the major discovery or discoveries made by each student contributor (or researcher) and the procedure that each group member will follow both during the period of investigation and during any inquiries that still need to be pursued.

The Research Team Feedback Form does not follow a traditional fill-in-the-blanks format. Instead it offers students opportunities to call on or to develop their own creativity within a given structure. The form also allows a teacher to quickly discern or assess the relevance and accuracy of each student's response(s) as well as offering a greater probability of knowing who has actually contributed and who has not. (Students are reminded that the back of the form is available for additional notations that need to be made to give the teacher a clear understanding of their contributions and accomplishments. Students are also instructed to attach actual notes or reports developed during the lesson as evidence of their participation.) For each investigation, a new form is provided for the group and, at the beginning of the activity, the specific focus for the group is refined to reflect what has been accomplished and any changes in what needs to be completed.

Performance Assessment Tasks

An additional important step in the inquiry/discovery lesson process is a post-activity assessment of student learning. That is, To what extent are students generating inquiries that can be used as the basis for assessing themselves? How might these inquiries be adapted to accurately reflect the learning that has occurred? Too often in science investigations, assessment is based on a generic lab report that does not adequately demonstrate individual inquiries or discoveries, especially if students merely copy each other's notes. One of the more distinctive assessment practices in inquiry/discovery instruction is use of "performance tasks." Such tasks can be designed to assess both content understanding and skill learning based on each student's ability to generate questions, manipulate data, and draw conclusions based on evidence. Following is an example of a performance assessment component to be used following the Archimedes investigation described earlier.

Sample Performance Assessment Task: Archimedes Investigation

From the experience you had during the sinking boat demonstration, devise two ways to determine the volume of air inside the "boat." Compare the results obtained by each of these methods.

1. Defend or dispute the fact that a boat floating on water has an apparent mass of 0 grams.

2. Describe how Archimedes could have proven, using his understanding or principle, that his king's crown was made from a metal or metals other than pure gold.

3. Develop a further question or inquiry related to information you have heard or observed about floating and sinking objects.

Note that this assessment does not take the form of teacher-constructed questions, nor does it ask for a summation of what has been observed during the activities. Instead, it enables students to demonstrate both content understanding and skill learning and allows for a variety of responses through which the students demonstrate strengths (parts of the investigation they are most comfortable with) and areas in which they might still have questions to be resolved. Compared with a conventional test, this type of assessment can offer a deeper and more powerful picture of student learning.

Summary

To summarize, teachers are encouraged to keep the following principles in mind as they design and conduct lessons for promoting student-oriented inquiry/discovery learning in science:

Principles for Lesson Planning

1. Activities should enable students to develop and practice higher levels of conceptual thinking by directly involving them in hands-on investigations in which they collect evidence and draw conclusions.

2. Learning is best accomplished by having students focus (over an extended period of time) on particular concepts in depth and their related ideas over an even more extended period of time.

3. Investigations followed by discussion and further exploration and discovery are necessary if students are to acquire the focus and concentration needed both to increase content understanding and to develop scientific thinking skills.

4. "Flashy" demonstrations or demonstrations that produce unexpected results can serve to motivate students to pursue further learning. However, demonstrations presented as components of lectures in place of hands-on, laboratory-based investigations are of limited effectiveness in promoting long-term learning and behavioral changes.

5. Although inquiry and discovery skills are best developed through science instruction during which students collect evidence and draw conclusions, these same skills should also be strengthened through appropriately designed experiences in other academic areas, such as language and mathematics.

6. Assessment of student participation and learning should be an integral component of instruction, not simply an afterthought.

Chapter 3

Introducing and Planning Inquiry/Discovery Lessons

AS EXPLAINED IN PREVIOUS CHAPTERS, the inquiry/discovery approach develops skills in scientific thinking, reasoning, and practice by encouraging students to take more active and responsible roles in the various phases of science investigations. Although it is laudatory to set the goal of fostering greater responsibility within students themselves for their learning, there is need to provide adequate preparation and grounding for instruction that meets this goal. The continuing issue of whether we are teachers of subject matter or teachers of students comes to mind here. We, as teachers, often feel so overwhelmed by the pressures of "covering" the content that it is tempting to discount our responsibility to develop the habits of mind that will be required of our students in the twenty-first century. The key to success in inquiry/discovery instruction is in understanding that new levels of skill and responsibility can be introduced to students in stages, over time. However, the decision as to when and how to move students to the next level of responsibility should not be a matter of guesswork. With the support of the tools introduced in this chapter, you will find that it is possible to design well-conceived instructional sequences that enable students to develop increasing levels of skill and proficiency in their science learning. Use of these tools can assist you in structuring lessons that address and eventually meet state-based science content standards as well as the Inquiry Standards proposed by the National Research Council (2000). Most important, you will be able to cultivate the student enthusiasm that results in both effective learning and sustained lifelong interest in science as a possible career.

Building "Rigor" into Science Learning

Prompted by the National Science Education Standards, there is increasing emphasis on building "rigor" into science learning. In the view of many science educators, including textbook authors, increasing the "rigor" in instruction means that students should be expected to memorize more complex and advanced levels of content at lower and lower grade levels. In our view, this conception of "rigor" is self-defeating. Excessive memorization of content often leads to little to no increase in student understanding. Instead, instruction designed to elicit student questioning or inquiry coupled with the discovery of new relationships, interconnections, and applications among the topics of study is a more effective measure of "rigor," regardless of the grade level. Inquiry/discovery opportunities lead students to desire to learn more and enable them to better understand the multiple aspects of the science being taught, and thus to retain more of the content. Furthermore, the emphasis on developing students' critical thinking and "process" skills offers them better preparation for succeeding in college-level science. Consequently, it is our responsibility, as science teachers, to adopt this "more rigorous" approach to instruction and to plan accordingly. Many of the lesson sequences described in this book demonstrate a healthy degree of "rigor" as we have defined it.

Understanding Levels of Student Responsibility: The Instructional Matrix

In conventional science instruction the teacher orchestrates the entire process from determining the topic of study and the directions for the "laboratory" procedure to conducting the investigation (if this actually occurs) and summarizing the conclusions and applications. In inquiry/discovery instruction the teacher's role shifts gradually over time so that the students—over the course of a year and from grade to grade—assume more and more responsibility for initiating, carrying out, and following up with investigative experiences.

Our experience indicates that students are enthused about inquiry/ discovery practices, and, as they gain in skill and proficiency, become more eager to take on greater degrees of responsibility and challenge. As explained earlier, changes in the students' roles should occur gradually, on the basis of their level of readiness. For the teacher, the significant question is when and where in the science lesson sequence is it appropriate to introduce students to new levels of skill and responsibility. As noted in Chapter Two, inquiry/discovery lessons typically include five steps within the following three phases:

Pre-Laboratory Phase

1. *Inquiry:* Problem or topic is proposed for exploration.

2. *Method:* Investigative procedure is planned.

Laboratory Phase

3. *Investigation:* Activity or experiment is carried out.

   • Evidence or data are collected or observed.

   • Data or results are analyzed.

Post-Laboratory Phase

4. *Conclusions:* Answers or explanations are summarized.

5. *Extension:* Applications are discussed and related inquiries are explored or investigated.

On the basis of our experience, the *extension* segment (Stage 5 in the Post-Laboratory phase) is the most comfortable or natural time to introduce students to inquiry/discovery practices. Whether the lesson involves a teacher-performed demonstration or a highly scripted laboratory experiment, it is after an investigation has been concluded that teachers are most used to inviting students to consider the implications and applications of the findings. Students should be encouraged to discuss and inquire about investigative outcomes; too often conventional instruction does not provide this opportunity. Students who are new to the inquiry process may require special support from teachers at this stage in formulating higher-order questions or in analyzing "cause and effect" relationships. (Strategies to support students in developing "inference" skills will be addressed in more detail in Chapter Six.)

As students gain experience and skill in discussing real-world implications, and applications, of investigative findings, they can be encouraged to take more active roles during the earlier stages of a lesson. This would include taking initiative in explaining the conclusions and results of an investigation (Stage 4); conducting an investigative activity independently, sometimes with the support of other students and with the teacher's oversight (Stage 3); planning an investigative procedure themselves (Stage 2); and eventually proposing an area of study or a research problem on their own (Stage 1).

In Table 3.1, the Levels of Inquiry/Discovery Instructional Matrix (also referred to as the Instructional Matrix), we summarize six potential levels of "challenge" to be considered in designing inquiry/discovery lesson sequences (or lesson units). Corresponding to the three-phase lesson format outlined earlier, the Instructional Matrix identifies points in the

TABLE 3.1

The Levels of Inquiry/Discovery Instructional Matrix.

| Levels of Inquiry/ Discovery | Pre-Laboratory Experience | | Laboratory Experience | Post-Laboratory Experience | |
	Proposes Problem or Issue to Be Explored	Plans Procedure to Be Used to Explore	Carries Out Procedures, Collects and Analyzes Data from Observations	Supplies Answers or Conclusions Related to the Inquiry	Considers How the Discoveries Can Be Applied or Can Lead to Other Inquiries
0	Teacher	Teacher	Teacher	Teacher	Teacher
1	Teacher	Teacher	Teacher	Teacher	Students
2	Teacher	Teacher	Teacher	Students	Students
3	Teacher	Teacher	Students	Students	Students
4	Teacher	Students	Students	Students	Students
5	Students	Students	Students	Students	Students

Source: This matrix was originally presented at the August 2, 2000, Biennial Conference on Chemical Education at the University of Michigan by Francis X. Sutman and Joseph S. Schmuckler.

lesson sequence at which students can be encouraged, with the teacher's guidance, to take primary responsibility. In Level 0 instruction, students have no active role at all in the entire lesson (this represents conventional "didactic" teaching). However, with Level 1 instruction, the students take a lead in Stage 5 of the Post-Laboratory phase (consider applications). This is often an "extension" activity whereby students may explore how the investigative findings link to the real world; very often this "discovery" step leads to further research or inquiries. As the students develop in capability, they can take on Level 2 instruction, whereby they learn how to explain investigative outcomes and results (supply conclusions). Once the students gain skills from participating in the Post-Laboratory phase of a lesson, they can be encouraged to take the lead in the Laboratory phase, whereby they conduct investigations (carry out the experiment). At this stage, students independently or in teams collect and observe scientific data and very often are required to use mathematics, graphic representations, or other tools for presenting their evidence. Eventually, with appropriate scaffolding, students can progress to Level 4 instruction, whereby they design the investigative activity largely on their own (plan the procedure). And, finally, students can participate in all Levels including Level 5 instruction, whereby they are encouraged to propose inquiries or topics worthy of formal investigative study (propose the problem). Instruction at Levels 4 and 5 most often applies to students at the high school level, but as we shall see, middle school students can and occasionally do take initiative in the Pre-Laboratory phase, whereby they pose a research problem on their own.

The determination of an appropriate instructional level is based on the degree of responsibility and skill development that is to be expected of students and also on the students' level of preparedness. (In Chapter Seven we offer suggestions for assessing the students' participation in inquiry/discovery activities, including their readiness to take on new challenges.) Teachers will need to support and scaffold students carefully as they progress, but eventually the students will gain in skill and proficiency and, ultimately, are likely to perform better in meeting national standards for both content and inquiry learning.

Enabling students to gradually assume independent roles during every stage of a science lesson is a central goal of inquiry/discovery instruction. However, instruction at Levels 4 and 5 is realistic and appropriate, with few exceptions, only for students enrolled in advanced placement high school–level and college-level science courses. For middle school students, instruction at Level 2 or perhaps Level 3 usually offers the appropriate challenge. High school students, however, should be able to function comfortably at Level 3 and, at times, Level 4. That is, high school students should routinely be offered major responsibility for carrying out laboratory procedures, supplying answers or discoveries, and considering the implications of what they have discovered.

The Instructional Matrix in Planning Science Lessons

What does it mean to teach at differing levels of inquiry/discovery? To address this question, we present scenarios of three different approaches to a science lesson, each designed to introduce the concept of "momentum" to middle school students. We will then examine each lesson in light of the challenge and skill-learning opportunities offered to the students. To begin, we will describe a more conventional lesson that due to its didactic approach would be considered Level 0 inquiry/discovery instruction.

Level 0 Lesson (Study of Momentum)

Time Line: 1 class period

Student Learning Objectives:

- To understand the nature of momentum

- To enhance reading and mathematics skills

Materials: Textbook, chalk, chalkboard

The teacher begins this lesson at the end of a class period by directing the students to read, as an out-of-school assignment, the textbook section related to the concept of momentum. The next day, he goes over the content in the textbook with the students. For example, he reviews the definition for momentum, relating it to mass and velocity. This calls for redefinition of those two terms, taught earlier in the week. The teacher writes the definitions for mass and velocity on the chalkboard while repeating the definitions orally, and he calls on several students to repeat these definitions as well. Many students copy down the definitions in their notebooks.

The teacher then asks individual students various questions that he assumes they can answer from having completed their previous reading assignments. For example, he asks, "What will happen to the momentum of an object if its velocity is doubled and the mass remains constant?" "What is the difference between speed and velocity?" "What are the metric units of measure for momentum?" The students are unable to answer most of these questions. The teacher grumbles about their lack of preparedness and answers the questions himself!

At this point, the teacher refers the students to the problems related to momentum included at the end of the textbook chapter. Most of the remaining instructional time is spent on practice solving these problems using the "plug in" formula from the textbook. The teacher moves about the room checking the students' work. Toward the end of the class the teacher briefly touches on a few examples related to the importance of understanding momentum and its applications in everyday life. The most significant example is given by the teacher. He urges students to consider the momentum of moving cars, which, depending on the velocity, causes them to travel a considerable distance once the brakes are applied; thus the need to keep "safe distances" between cars moving one in front of the other to prevent rear-end collisions.

Comments on Level 0 Lesson (Study of Momentum)

During this lesson, we saw that students were involved in reading, listening to the teacher lecture, solving math problems, and perhaps copying down information that had either been presented by the teacher or read from the textbook. The students were generally on task, although several appeared to be bored or disinterested. What was missing? To what degree would any of this have been memorable, even engrossing? Where was the active interaction between students and content? Such an approach to instruction is unlikely to result in a positive, memorable experience for students, mainly because it offers neither students nor teacher opportunities to challenge or expand on the ideas presented. Students were not given a chance to inquire or take initiative in any part of the lesson; their role was entirely reactive. In only one instance was an appropriate application to a basic science principle addressed, and this was presented by the teacher. Therefore, at best, this lesson meets the criteria for inquiry/discovery at level 0, according to the Instructional Matrix.

How might this lesson have been modified to create a Level 1 lesson, also on the topic of momentum? In the following example, we will look at how a teacher (one of our contributors) transformed a Level 0 lesson into Level 1 instruction by adding new elements.

Level 1 Lesson (Study of Momentum)

Time Line: 2 class periods
Student Learning Objectives:

- To learn the meaning of physical momentum: ($P = m \times v$)
- To understand the impact that changes in velocity have on the momentum of a given mass
- To consider applications of momentum

Materials: A six-to-eight-foot-long smooth board, two chairs of different heights on which one of the ends of the board can rest, a medium-size cart with wheels, an appropriate-size block of wood that weighs an amount that can be moved by the rolling car, a meter stick, a textbook, chalk, a chalkboard, and a PowerPoint presentation.

The teacher introduces students to the concept of momentum by asking the question, "What do you think is meant by the term *momentum*?" Receiving no answer from the students, this teacher defines the term *momentum* and writes it on the board as follows: "The momentum of an object is its mass multiplied by the velocity at which it is moving. We represent this by the following formula: $P = m \times v$." He then explains that he will demonstrate how momentum works. "You will observe the result of momentum as I allow this cart to freely roll down this board, which is leaning against a chair with the opposite end resting on the floor. I will now place a block of wood on the floor at one end of the inclined board." Then the teacher asks, "What do you think will happen to the block of wood?" He receives three responses from the students. "I think the block will stop the moving cart." "No, the cart will push the block of wood across the floor." "I don't know what will happen."

The cart is allowed to roll down the inclined board and hit the wooden block, pushing the block some distance across the floor. Using a meter stick the teacher determines that the block was pushed forward a distance of 26 cm. "Let's try this again," the teacher says, "after I rest the one end of the board onto a higher chair." This second trial results in the block of wood moving 36 cm across the floor. The teacher explains that "the 10 cm increase in distance results from an increase in the momentum of the cart, because of an increase in its velocity. Even though the mass of the cart did not change, its velocity increased because we increased the slope of the board. In both cases, all of the momentum of the cart was transmitted to the block of wood. Scientists refer to the transfer of momentum from one object to another as the 'conservation of momentum'."

Following this demonstration, the teacher explains how to solve the first three problems related to momentum at the end of the chapter in the science textbook, using the formula $P = m \times v$. At the end of the class period, the teacher assigns students to read the momentum chapter in the textbook and to solve the six remaining problems at the end of the chapter preparing for review during the next class period.

During the next class period, the teacher reviews the assigned problems by calling on individual students to explain how they obtained their solutions. He follows this by inviting students to discuss some real-life applications of momentum. Students are initially hesitant. To prompt their thinking, he conducts a brief PowerPoint presentation featuring photographs of situations involving momentum. For example, a highway with grade warnings, a runaway truck ramp, and a warning sign that says, "Keep at least 100 feet between your car and the one in front of you."

These examples do initiate student questions, comments, and discussion. For example, one student asks, "What is meant by the grade of a hill?" Another student comments, "The test for a state driver's license expects you to know how much space to leave between the car you are driving and the one that is in front of you at speeds of 35, 45, and 55 miles per hour in order to prevent rear-end collisions." A third student asks, "Why are stop ramps on downhill roads needed for trucks and not cars?" Students refer to other examples as well, including questions about the safety of using skateboards on steep slopes.

Following this brief discussion the remaining math problems from the text are reviewed, and students ask the usual question: What will appear on the test to be given on the following day?

Comments on Level 1 Lesson (Study of Momentum)

In this lesson, we note that the students were offered no opportunity to decide on the content to be studied or how the topic should be investigated.

Although the demonstration conducted by the teacher enriched the lesson somewhat, the teacher took full responsibility for planning the activity and carrying it out, including conducting the measurements. What distinguished this lesson from the preceding Level 0 lesson was the extension segment in which students were encouraged to become truly involved in considering some applications of momentum as well as implications. The teacher developed enough structure (initiating and directing the activity itself) for the inexperienced students, so that the comfort level remained high for the students, allowing them to link what they learned in the lesson to real-world situations. On the basis of this analysis, the instruction meets the criteria for Level 1 of inquiry/discovery according to the Instructional Matrix.

It should be noted there were two weaknesses in the teacher's approach. The first of these was use of the phrase "What do you think (in this case) momentum means?" Use of this phrase is ineffective because any responses to questions worded in this way are always correct. That which students *think* is the answer is not what teachers should be seeking in science classes. Instead, the teacher's role is to support students in searching for appropriate answers to questions that are based on what students have actually experienced. Teachers would do better to ask, for example, "Considering our recent experience in the laboratory, what is ...?" Or "Considering what we have just read, what is ...?"

The second concern is that the teacher asked students to *guess* what the results would be as the cart rolls down the incline. Simple guessing usually has no place in science instruction. Hypothesizing, based on evidence from past experience(s), is the strategy or approach that should be emphasized. To meet this approach, the teacher might have proposed, "Let's see what happens as the ..." Or, calling upon a particular student, he could have asked, "Could you predict what will happen, and if so, on what basis did you make your prediction?"

We turn now to a third lesson on this same topic of momentum that is designed to emphasize the next higher level of inquiry/discovery learning. Except for a few additional tools, the instructional setup and materials are very similar to that of the previous investigation.

Level 2 Lesson (Study of Momentum)

Time Line: 3 to 4 class periods
Student Learning Objectives:

- To develop a more in-depth understanding of momentum, including related concepts of velocity and mass

- To develop skills in recording and tabulating data and in formulating conclusions from experimental data

- To consider applications based on the concept of momentum

Materials: An office-type chair that can be raised and lowered to different heights, a large protractor, a six-to-eight-foot-long board, a medium-size cart with low-friction wheels, an appropriate block of wood, a meter stick, a stopwatch, graph paper, and a PowerPoint presentation that includes the usual applications related to momentum.

Pre-Laboratory Phase: The teacher introduces the topic of momentum toward the end of the instructional period by using a PowerPoint presentation to offer students opportunities to visualize applications of the concept: Some examples include pounding pilings into beds of sand for building purposes, rear-end collisions of automobiles, and bowling. The teacher then assigns, as an out-of-school activity, students to read from their textbook about momentum and also to visit Websites on the "momentum equation" via Google links and then, from these sources, to find and compare the definitions for *momentum*, as the term is used by physicists. They are then to search for the equation used to determine the momentum of moving objects and to designate two applications of momentum beyond those presented in the PowerPoint presentation. In addition, each student is to come to class with at least one written question or inquiry about the nature of momentum.

On the following day, the teacher begins instruction by determining if each student has constructed a question for later consideration. Some of the inquiries still use the term *momentum* in its informal sense. The teacher helps the class focus on the meaning as used by physicists. One of the more fruitful questions developed by a student is, "Is time ever taken into account in considering momentum?" Each student is asked to read his or her inquiry to the class and place it on the query board.

The teacher then proceeds to conduct a demonstration of the investigation method, announcing that the results will give an indication of momentum and its relation to velocity. Resting the long board against a chair at an incline of about 20 degrees and placing a block of wood at the foot of the board, she enables students to observe as a cart rolls down the board and collides with the wooden block, pushing the block some distance across the floor. Using a meter stick, she measures the distance the block is pushed. The teacher repeats this same action but uses a stopwatch to measure the time the cart takes from the starting point to reach its point of impact. She then gives students copies of printed directions to follow while the same procedure is conducted at progressively steeper levels of incline (30, 40, 50, and 60 degrees). The directions specify that students are to conduct three trials at each of the four differing angles of incline and to collect data on the distance and time measurements for each trial. The results at each angle are then to be averaged and the average values plotted on a graph. Each student is then to develop written conclusions from the investigation based on analysis of the data collected.

Before starting the trials, the teacher calls on individual students to review segments of the directions orally for the class and invites questions regarding the procedure. A few students ask why three trials are needed for each level of incline. The teacher invites other students to offer answers to this question, but not receiving any responses suggests that the answers will become clear as the investigation unfolds.

Laboratory Phase: As the investigation begins, the teacher calls for student volunteers to participate in various aspects of the procedure. One student raises the height of the chair while the teacher uses the large protractor to increase the angle of the board's incline. Another student volunteers to start the cart rolling down the board. Additional students take turns measuring the cart's travel time using the stopwatch, in measuring the distance the wooden block is pushed using the meter stick, in recording the results for each trial, and in calculating average values to be noted in a table the teacher has drawn on the chalkboard. Following the directions, each student records all of the time and distance measurement data collected, including the average values, in his or her lab notebooks. After all of the trials have been run, each student prepares a graphic representation of the results indicating the average distances the block is pushed (the dependent variable) plotted against the independent (or controlled) variable, the angle of the slope. Another curve is plotted against the average time differences at each trial.

Post-Laboratory Phase: Following preparation of the graphs, the teacher invites students to discuss what their graphic representations mean, drawing from what they have already read about the momentum concept. Examining the plotted averages and the curves drawn from them, the students comment that there seems to be a direct relationship between increase in angle of the board and the distance the wooden block is pushed upon impact. The greater the slope, the greater the distance the block travels. Students also note that as the angle of incline increases, the time it takes for the cart to roll down the incline decreases, even though distance and mass remain the same. These observations lead students, through discussion, to draw three conclusions: (1) the cart must accelerate or increase in speed or velocity as it moves down the slope, because, after all, it begins at 0 speed; (2) the average speed and final speed (or velocity) must increase in direct proportion to the angle of slope, because the cart takes less time to travel the same distance at each increase in angle; and (3) the momentum transmitted from the moving cart to the wooden block must depend heavily on the speed (velocity) of the moving cart, because the "mass" of the cart remains the same from one trial to the next. With the teacher's prompting and support, the students eventually come to realize that their graphic representations are linked to the formula for calculating the physical momentum of a moving object: momentum = mass × velocity $(P = m \times v)$.

Arriving at this conclusion, one student asks what the result would be at different angles of incline, say with the ramp at a 55-degree angle. The teacher encourages students to predict the results based on interpolation of the data from their graphs, taking care to explain the meaning of *interpolation*. Time is taken to complete the interpolation or predicted value, and it proves to be reasonably correct when confirmed by the repeated trials. Another student asks how the results would differ if the cart was heavier. The teacher compliments the student on the question and suggests that he post it on the query board, so that students might try conducting additional trials on their own using differently weighted carts as a follow-up investigation later on. At this stage, the students are encouraged to write up an explanation for momentum developed from the results of various trials and to record the data and results in their laboratory notebooks, completing the task as a homework assignment, if necessary.

As an additional out-of-school assignment, the teacher asks students to study the mathematical problems and other questions at the end of the chapter on momentum in their science textbook. But rather than having students complete and solve the math problems on their own, the teacher gives each student a sheet containing written solutions to all but one of the problems. On the following day, the teacher calls on individual students to orally explain the process by which each has obtained the answer to the problem. Only where the solution is not clearly understood by the students does the teacher assist with an explanation. Following discussion of the math problems, students are invited to briefly summarize what they learned about momentum from the lesson. The teacher then collects the students' laboratory notebooks, indicating that she would be grading the clarity of the data records and graphs prepared from the data as well as the written summary reports.

As an extension activity, the teacher invites students to think of possible safety issues involving momentum right on the school campus. Students immediately mention the various ramps used by people in wheelchairs to access the building, by the maintenance staff for transporting heavy equipment on carts, and of course surreptitiously by skateboarders. The teacher assigns teams to study the ramps and write a brief report analyzing the potential safety hazards. The team reports focus on the degree of slope of each ramp, the types of vehicles used including the adequacy of their braking systems, and the weights carried (people, furniture), all in relation to momentum. The maintenance staff is helpful in assisting students with completing their reports. In a follow-up discovery activity, the maintenance staff agrees to show students a new electrical generator recently purchased by the school district. By including an unbalanced flywheel, the new generator is capable of producing electricity at 25 percent greater efficiency than was true for the older generator. To prepare students for understanding this application of momentum, the teacher duplicates an article from the January-February 2007 issue of *American Scientist* journal titled "Getting All Revved Up." The article explains how an electrical generator can be designed to store energy in the form of momentum by distributing the mass of the flywheel unevenly instead of uniformly, thus increasing the efficiency of electricity production.

Comments on Level 2 Lesson (Study of Momentum)

In the lesson sequence just described, we note that the students were not expected to decide on the problem to be explored or to plan the procedure for investigating the topic. However, the teacher did design the investigation so that the students were partially responsible for carrying out the procedure and for collecting and tabulating the data. The task of plotting the data graphically and analyzing the results offered students an opportunity to practice a skill frequently called on by scientists. Through collective discussion of the visual graphic representations, students were able to better connect what they had read about momentum to their investigative findings. By noting how the increases in velocity of the cart changed the distance the wooden block was pushed upon impact, the students, with the teacher's guidance, were able to arrive at a more detailed understanding of momentum and its relationship to mass and velocity than had they merely read about the topic in their textbook. In the follow-up sequence regarding the mathematical problems, the teacher distributed solutions to the problems and invited students to discuss the solutions collectively rather than expecting students to work out every problem on their own as a homework assignment. Because students very often do not complete homework assignments involving math problems, the practice of having them explain the mathematical solutions orally in class helps to ensure that they better understand the formulas and processes used and how they connect to the content. Research conducted by A. Borawec in 1968 suggests that this practice results in students achieving better scores on classroom-administered tests. Another advantage is that it conserves valuable instructional time that can be better devoted to involvement in hands-on investigations.

The final step in this lesson was distinctive in that students were given responsibility to explore a real-world application of momentum, including analyzing a problem and preparing a written report. It should also be noted that the lesson was introduced with examples of real-world applications and that students were given a "discovery" activity at the outset whereby they were encouraged to compare definitions, research formulas, and identify additional applications. Collectively, all of these activities, especially the investigation itself, helped to develop the students' conceptual understanding of the content as well as their inquiry/discovery skills. Overall, we can conclude that this lesson is easily classified at Level 2 according to the Instructional Matrix.

In the next lesson we focus on an extended understanding of momentum as it relates to acceleration and offer an example of an instructional Level 3 lesson. Because the level of understanding and skill demanded of the students is more challenging or rigorous than that required in carrying out the previous lessons, this lesson is designed for instruction with a more experienced high school science class.

Level 3 Lesson (Study of Momentum)

Time Line: 3 class periods, and out-of-school activity
Student Learning Objectives:

- To gain extended understanding of physical momentum and related concepts of velocity and mass

- To gain skills in investigative practices, including skills in conducting measurements, in analyzing data, and in drawing conclusions based on data

- To gain skill in plotting graphs from collected data and in making predictions from plotted curves of collected data

Materials: Enough of each of the following materials and equipment for use by teams of three to five students each: commercial inclined planes with attached protractor, small low-friction rolling carts, blocks of wood each having the same appropriate mass, meter sticks, laboratory tables or other flat desks that can be moved together to allow carts and wooden blocks to travel some distance without falling to the floor, balances (for determining weights or masses of wooden blocks), speed or velocity detectors (available through the Discovery Channel Store Website, www.discoverystore.com), graph paper, laboratory notebooks, textbook, access to Websites about momentum, and other appropriate hardcopy references.

Pre-Laboratory Phase: The problem or topic of study of this lesson is not specifically stated. Instead, the teacher prepares written directions and distributes a copy to each student. Dividing the class into teams of three to five students each, the teacher gives each team a set of the investigative materials and then calls on one member of each team to read the directions orally to the other team members, clarifying procedural questions as necessary. The directions call for students to study the "behavior" of the cart as it travels down the full length of the inclined plane, set at varying degrees of slope (30, 40, 50, and 60 degrees) and allowed to collide with the block of wood that has been placed at the base of the incline. Three trials are to be conducted for each angle of incline and the results averaged. The directions also call for each student to prepare a graph plotting the average values and to record this in his or her laboratory notebook.

Laboratory Phase: Taking care to start the cart rolling at the appropriate point, the students use a speed or velocity detector to measure the cart's velocity just before it collides with the wooden block. They also measure the distance the block is pushed upon impact and record the results. After conducting three trials for each angle of incline and calculating the averages, each student prepares two graphs of the team's data indicating (1) the average velocity of the cart plotted against each corresponding angle of incline and (2) the average distance the block moves against each corresponding angle of incline.

Post-Laboratory Phase: Once the graphs have been completed, the students are encouraged to display their graphs to the class and to discuss what the data suggest. Examining the graphs, students immediately note that the averages among teams vary slightly and ask why this is so, even though each team has followed the same directions using similar equipment. The teacher supports students in explaining typical causes for such "errors" and how they can be adjusted for mathematically, noting that there could have been slight differences in the weights of the carts and the wooden block as well as inaccuracies in measurement. Focusing on the graphs that appear to be most alike based on their average values for velocities, the students comment on what appears to be a proportional relationship between the steepness of the angle of the incline and the distance the block is pushed upon impact. At this point, the teacher encourages students to pursue an explanation for this relationship by assigning them individually to read the chapter on momentum in their textbook and also to visit Websites or consult other references related to physical momentum, and to report back on their findings during the next class. In conducting this research task, students eventually discover the momentum formula: $P = m \times v$ (P = Momentum, m = mass, v = velocity). Following the class discussion the next day, the teacher assigns each student to prepare a written summary of what they have learned about momentum in their laboratory notebooks, including an explanation of how it links to their investigative results and graphic representation.

Extension: To further confirm their understanding of physical momentum, each team is assigned the task of designing three inquiries related to the investigation and to discover the answers, completing the work outside of class, if necessary. Students are also to investigate unusual applications of momentum. Each student, in turn, is expected to record the team's inquiries, findings, and explanations on his or her final report due at the end of the lessons. Following are examples of the team inquiries and responses:

- From our graphs, can we determine the distance the wooden block will move upon impact if hit by the cart rolling down a 70-degree slope? (The curve drawn on the graph for the collected data can be extrapolated beyond the point representing distance traveled beyond the 60-degree incline. Similar extrapolation can be made beyond the 70-degree incline if the graph has been designed to include these projected values.)

- Can we make an accurate prediction for slope angles of less than 60 degrees, for example, a slope of 45 degrees? (The velocity at impact obtained when the slope is less than 60 degrees can be determined by interpolation using an earlier drawn curve.)

- Do speed and velocity mean the same thing? (No. Speed is the distance traveled during a given unit of time; for example, cm/sec. Velocity is the distance traveled by an object during a given unit of time in a specific direction, for example: cm/sec west. Planets and moons travel in orbits at given velocities because their direction of motion constantly changes. Therefore, though velocity changes, the speed may not.)

- What change in momentum would occur if a block with double the mass of the earlier block was used? (All distances traveled by the block would be half that of each distance at a given angle.)

- What would result if the weight of the cart was doubled? (The momentum would double.)

Assessment: In reviewing the laboratory reports several days later, the teacher bases the grading on accuracy and care in presentation of data (tables clearly organized; graphs correctly drawn, labeled, and titled). He also looks for a detailed summary of what the student learned both from the investigation itself and from the team's follow-up activity, including a list of the references consulted, all of it providing evidence that the momentum concept was clearly understood. Several of the students' reports mentioned unusual examples of momentum, including the use of momentum measurements to determine the mass of subatomic particles, to test the effectiveness of new auto airbag designs, to estimate effective payloads for space vehicles, to plan for conserving fuel in commercial aircraft, and to predict the potential damage of tsunamis after earthquakes.

Comments on Level 3 Lesson (Study of Momentum)

In analyzing this lesson, we note that the teacher decided on the topic to be studied and planned the procedure to be followed. However, the students were given minimal introduction and directions, and were fully in charge of carrying out the investigation. They also designed their own approaches for answering inquiries raised in the extension segment. The lesson was structured to encourage students to compare data and question the investigative results, engaging them in a form of critical analysis that is vital to the scientific process. In this regard, the lesson also helped students understand the importance of accuracy in conducting and recording measurements as well as the need for verifying scientific findings (or replicating experiments) before valid conclusions can be drawn. A distinctive feature of this lesson is that students read about the momentum concept only after the investigation was performed. Students challenged to explain investigative findings on their own often end up exploring the topic in greater depth, which enables them to retain more of the content, including the mathematical processes. The task of requiring students to construct research questions and answer them developed their conceptual understanding (and mathematical competence) even further. In this type of lesson, the quality of the follow-up inquiries can be taken into account in the final grading of each student's effort and output. Considering the responsibilities and opportunities given to the students, this lesson can easily be classified as Level 3 according to the Instructional Matrix.

Designing Inquiry/Discovery Lesson Sequences

Now that we have explored how to increase the level of rigor and student responsibility in a science lesson, we will look at how specific lesson plans and instructional strategies can be modified to effectively enhance inquiry/discovery learning. In Table 3.2, we present a rubric

TABLE 3.2

Planning Rubric for Inquiry/Discovery Science Lessons.

Level 0	Teacher/Student Roles
Inquiry	Teacher designates problem or issue to be studied.
Method	Teacher identifies specific available procedure and the equipment to be used.
Investigation	Teacher demonstrates procedure with students functioning as observers or assistants.
Conclusions	Teacher supplies answers and conclusions, usually ahead of time.
Extension	Teacher limits follow-up activity to student discussion of outcomes.
Level 1	
Inquiry	Teacher invites students to study a predetermined problem, pointing them to resources.
Method	Teacher designates experimental procedure and equipment that students will use.
Investigation	Teacher guides students throughout the procedure; indicates what the conclusions should be; may demonstrate the investigation.
Conclusions	Teacher designates answers (observations and conclusions) for students to write.
Extension	*Students* are encouraged to suggest applications or implications based on the outcomes.
Level 2	
Inquiry	Teacher leads students in discussion of a predetermined problem, pointing them to resources only if necessary.
Method	Teacher leads students in discussion of predetermined procedure.
Investigation	Teacher closely monitors students as *they* carry out activity, providing clarification as needed.
Conclusions	*Students* discuss predetermined conclusions to the inquiry with the teacher's guidance.
Extension	*Students* identify applications or follow-up inquiries with the teacher's support.
Level 3	
Inquiry	Teacher supplies problems or encourages students to formulate problem, using their prior knowledge and earlier discoveries.
Method	Teacher identifies the problem and resources that students will use to plan the procedure.
Investigation	*Students* are encouraged to go beyond the initially set procedure as inquiry unfolds and discoveries develop.
Conclusions	*Students* derive "acceptable" outcomes and conclusions with the teacher's guidance.
Extension	*Students* identify applications and related inquiries with the teacher assisting only as needed.

TABLE 3.2

(Continued)

Level 4	Teacher/Student Roles
Inquiry	Teacher supplies problem or encourages students to formulate the problem by using written resources or prior knowledge.
Method	*Students* design the investigation with the teacher's mentoring and by using written resources.
Investigation	*Students* carry out the investigation individually or in groups with minimal teacher supervision, leading to discoveries.
Conclusions	*Students* generate their own answers and conclusions with limited assistance from the teacher.
Extension	*Students* independently investigate and present applications or follow-up inquiries.
Level 5	
Inquiry	*Students* initiate problem to be studied, possibly on the basis of earlier inquiries but not (overly) influenced by teacher.
Method	*Students* independently design the investigation, with procedures to be reviewed by the teacher.
Investigation	*Students* execute the investigation, independently gathering and organizing data and analyzing outcomes.
Conclusions	*Students* generate ideas from inquiry that may lead to discoveries beyond those anticipated by the teacher.
Extension	*Students* initiate open-ended discussion of applications and develop further inquiries.

designating appropriate roles and instructional strategies for typical steps in an inquiry/discovery-oriented lesson sequence. Corresponding to the Instructional Matrix (Table 3.1), the Planning Rubric embraces the five-part lesson sequence progressing from Level 0 to Level 5, showing how instructional strategies change based on shifts in teacher and student roles. The student roles, of course, become more prominent as the level of challenge increases. To understand how the Planning Rubric can be used in designing lesson sequences, we will examine a conventional lesson taught at Level 0 (case study description) and then suggest two plans for modifying the lesson in order to enhance students' level of understanding and skill development. All three lessons are in biology and focus on a study of insects for middle school–level students.

Level 0 Lesson (Study of Insects)

Time Line: 2 class periods

Student Learning Objectives:

- To gain an introductory understanding of insects and their general characteristics and development

- To be able to identify the four typical stages of insect development, and to name some of the external structures of a large variety of insects

Materials: Textbook, overhead transparencies

Introduction: The teacher initiates this lesson by giving students a homework assignment to read selected pages in their science textbook introducing them to the general characteristics of insects. During the next class period, the teacher calls on individual students to respond orally to his questions, the answers to which are included in the assigned text. Examples of these questions include the following:

- How many species of insects exist on Earth? How many individual insect organisms exist?

- What are some of the most common external features of insects?

- Name and describe each of the four stages of development of many insects.

- There is a picture of an adult grasshopper and mealworm in the chapter that you read for homework. How are the adult mealworm and grasshopper insects similar? In what ways do they differ?

The students do not respond well to the teacher's questions. When a student does respond, the teacher often repeats the answer. When no response is forthcoming, the teacher offers the answer himself, moving to the next question. Following this question-and-answer session, students are given another homework assignment to read the final six pages in the insect chapter. The next day the students come to class and listen to a lecture, during which the teacher repeats much of the content from their reading assignment. The lecture is supplemented with transparencies that display the external structure of the adult grasshopper, which the teacher describes as a typical insect. He also presents visuals depicting the external features of the mealworm at various stages of its development. This is followed by a short quiz, in which students are required to match different external structures across six different insects.

Comments on Level 0 Lesson (Study of Insects)

In this lesson, we note that all the activities were totally orchestrated by the teacher. Students were given no opportunities to inquire, much less discover through hands-on experiences, depending only on the textbook and the teacher's lectures as sources for information. The student's roles were completely passive; they simply listened to the teacher's lecture that repeated the content they had previously read. With the teacher asking students many recall-type questions, it's apparent that he valued repetition as it relates to learning and placed a strong emphasis on memorization. No time was devoted to follow-up discussion or to further exploration of the topic. Above all, there was no opportunity for students to practice any of the skills associated with inquiry/discovery. There is a significant negative result to this approach to instruction. Lecturing on the same content that appears in the textbook, if regularly practiced, can cause students not to take their out-of-school reading assignments seriously. Students catch on quickly!

In the next example, we present a plan for modifying this lesson, providing opportunity for inquiry/discovery learning at Level 1. Like the Level 0 lesson, this lesson also focuses on an introductory study of insects for the middle school classroom.

Level 1 Lesson (Study of Insects)

Time Line: 2 or 3 periods
Student Learning Objectives:

- To gain an introductory understanding of insects and their characteristics as called for in the National Science Education Standards for content learning

- To be able to identify the developmental stages of most insects, using the *Tennebrio Molitar* as an example

- To develop some experience in observation and recording of scientific data and in discussing the implications of investigative findings

Materials: A single mealworm culture housed in a plastic Petri dish (culture embeds all four stages of this insect's development in oatmeal flour, slightly moistened by a slice of apple), a hand lens for use by every two students, a small paint brush, forceps, small flat cookie-type pans, breathing masks for use by allergic-sensitive students, laboratory notebooks, a PowerPoint presentation on insect development and characteristics, and a biology textbook.

Pre-Laboratory Phase

- Introduce topic by inviting students to talk about what they know about "mealworms."

- Conduct a brief lecture and PowerPoint presentation describing the external structure of several insects, including the mealworm, and featuring the four typical stages of insect development, (egg, larva, pupa, and adult).

- Invite students to ask questions about the presentation, prompting them if necessary.

- Orally introduce students to investigative procedure, explaining that they are to observe the mealworm at its four stages of development and to make a drawing of each stage in their lab notebooks, labeling specific parts.

- Ensure that all students with allergies wear breathing masks, noting that they will be working with a live mealworm culture in oatmeal flour.

Laboratory Phase

- Diagram the four stages of mealworm development on the chalkboard and label them for students to refer to as they complete their drawings.

- Place examples of each stage of mealworm development on a cookie pan, using a paint brush and tweezers to uncover and remove specimens from the oatmeal flour.

- Distribute a hand lens to each team of two students.

- Enable students in pairs to briefly take turns in viewing and drawing the four stages of mealworm development.

Post-Laboratory Phase

- Invite students to share their drawings and talk about what they learned.

- Encourage students to ask questions about the mealworm or about insects, in general, prompting them as necessary. Post questions on the query board.

- Present a brief PowerPoint lecture summarizing developmental characteristics of the mealworm and comparing its characteristics to two other insects: the grasshopper and the ant. Emphasize that while many insects fly, the mealworm and the ant are exceptions. Introduce the mealworm's Latin or biological name, *Tennebrio Molitar*, explaining that the name indicates the organism's genus and species.

- Assign students to read textbook chapters about insects for homework; to be ready to answer questions at the end of the chapter during the following class period; and also to take time to polish and label their mealworm drawings, which will be graded.

- *Extension:* Invite students to talk about their experiences with insects, their likes, dislikes, or what they know about insects in general. Use the discussion to prompt further inquiries about the role of insects in the environment, including their harmful and beneficial impacts.

- *Assessment:* Grade students on their final lab drawings, on discussion participation and, eventually, with an end-of-unit quiz.

Comments on Level 1 Lesson Plan (Study of Insects)

Compared with the previous lesson, the learning experience is strengthened in this lesson plan by the addition of a hands-on activity, in which students are encouraged to observe an actual insect specimen and record their observations. Although direct observation is likely to be hampered by the limited availability of living specimens and time, the plan at least offers students some firsthand exposure to the developmental characteristics of an insect, making the textbook reading more relevant when it is assigned later in the lesson. Students can be carefully guided in the lab activity through the teacher's verbal directions. The teacher's diagram of the mealworm's developmental stages should support those students who may not be able to draw well or who may have insufficient time to observe the stages in detail. At the Post-Laboratory phase, we note that while the teacher summarizes the lesson, opportunity is provided for students to ask questions and discuss what they have learned. The extension segment also invites students to talk about their experiences with insects, providing opportunities for further discovery activities and serving to make this lesson more memorable than conventional "lecture and test" instruction. Student questions that typically surface in this lesson, when conducted at Level 1, include "Where are mealworms found in nature?" "Are they harmful to humans?" "Why is the apple needed in the culture?" "What does the Latin name mean?" "My grandmother often found worms in her flour bin. Should she have continued to use the flour?" "What do mealworms ordinarily eat?" "Where do they get water?" "What would happen if all insects disappeared from the environment?"

In the following example, we present yet a different lesson plan focusing again on an introductory study of insects for the middle school level. The lesson includes additional activities designed to further develop students' inquiry/discovery skills. Instruction is planned at Level 2 according to both the Instructional Matrix and the Planning Rubric, offering opportunities for students to develop conclusions and to consider the implications of their findings.

Level 2 Lesson (Study of Insects)

Time Line: 3 periods
Student Learning Objectives:

- To gain introductory understanding of insects and their external characteristics as called for in the National Science Education Standards

- To learn the developmental stages of many insects, using *Tennebrio Molitar* as a model

- To develop skills in the observation and recording of scientific data, and in developing accurate conclusions based on data

Materials: Same as those listed for the Level 1 lesson. However, to meet the learning objectives more effectively, sufficient mealworm cultures (in Petri dishes), lenses, and other materials are to be provided to facilitate students working in teams of two to three as they carry out the procedures; also breathing masks (for allergic or sensitive students), laboratory notebooks, a PowerPoint presentation describing external features of several insects, and at least one biology textbook. Websites about *Tennebrio Molitar* and several hardcopy references on insects, such as *Practical Entomology* by E. Bons (1992), should be readily available.

Pre-Laboratory Phase

- Invite students to talk about what they know about mealworms and also how they might go about learning more about mealworms and their characteristics.

- Prompt students, if necessary, as to the need for observing mealworms firsthand, not just reading about them.

- Provide each student with written directions for conducting an investigation of a mealworm culture: Each student team is to (1) search the culture for mealworms at four developmental stages using the tools provided; (2) draw and label the external features of mealworms at each stage; (3) refer to the textbook, Websites for mealworms, and printed references for identifying the stages, as necessary; and (4) develop two to three written inquiries that can be used as a basis for discussion following completion of the laboratory activity. Questions may be recorded on the Research Team Feedback Form.

- Divide the class into teams of two to three each and provide each team with a Petri dish culture and other materials, along with written directions for conducting the investigation. Provide masks as necessary.

Laboratory Phase

- Enable students to conduct observations (search for and isolate each stage of mealworm development, place each on tray, draw and label each stage; then return each specimen to the Petri dish) while referring to appropriate reference(s).

- Move from team to team to assist students in completing and labeling their drawings (allow them to complete the activity as a homework assignment, if necessary).

- Provide sufficient time (additional class periods, as necessary) for teams to complete inquiries, including opportunities to interact with one another in developing these.

Post-Laboratory Phase

- Encourage students to talk about what they learned from both their observations and related readings. Invite each team to present one inquiry, allowing time for discussion and responses.

- Conduct a brief PowerPoint presentation to summarize points about the role of insects in the environment (both harmful and beneficial).

- *Extension:* Assign students either to follow up on unanswered inquiries raised in class or to capture another species of insect "in the wild" and bring it to class with information they have gathered about the insect through Website or hardcover sources. (Return insects unharmed!)

- *Report:* Assign students to write a report of their laboratory experience, including their drawings, describing what they have learned about mealworms and other insects, and providing references.

- *Assessment:* Grade students based on their laboratory reports, discussion participation, and eventually on an end-of-unit quiz.

Comments on Level 2 Lesson (Study of Insects)

Compared with the plan for the previous lesson sequence, this plan offers students a richer learning experience leading to a better understanding of the content and the investigative process. Although the teacher decides on the topic to be explored and the investigative procedure, students are invited to talk about what they know about mealworms at the beginning of the lesson (a step usually revealing that they know very little) and are encouraged to think about how they might "study" such a specimen. Also, students are given full responsibility for carrying out the procedure under the teacher's guidance. In having enough available cultures for each student team, students should have greater opportunity to handle actual scientific specimens and to record their observations in detail. With the teacher refraining from assigning a textbook reading or providing a PowerPoint presentation about the topic at the Pre-Laboratory phase, students are given the more interesting experience of learning about mealworms on their own by consulting textbooks, Websites, or other resources to assist them in interpreting their observations. At this stage, students are often surprised to learn that mealworms are not "worms" but insects. They also discover the insect's scientific name, *Tennebrio Molitar*, and how this represents the genus and species. By requiring teams to develop questions for discussion at the Post-Laboratory phase, students are encouraged to read about insects in more detail, including consulting with one another, and are in a better position at the "conclusion" stage to discuss the role of insects in the environment, including how mealworms compare to other insects. Some teams may need more than a period or two to complete this process. And in the Laboratory phase, we note that students are even encouraged to complete their lab drawings (and write-ups) as an out-of-school assignment. This allows more time for classroom exploration and discussion about the topic and its implications. Past experience in conducting this lesson at Level 2 indicates that students become inspired enough to bring in other insects for study. Typical inquiries that arise include "Are we really looking at a larval stage, or is this simply a worm that got into the culture?" "Do mealworms, like bees and ants, live in cooperative colonies?" "Why do insects develop through four stages?" "Are there different species of mealworms?" "Do mealworms, like some mosquitoes, carry diseases?" "How do we reduce the spread of diseases carried by insects like lime ticks?" "Can 'bad' insects also be beneficial?" "How do mealworms (or other insects) react to pesticides?" "How many insects are there in the world?" These kinds of inquiries usually do not surface during Level 1 instruction.

Structuring Lessons to Best Meet the Potential of Students

When planning any science instruction, teachers need to make every effort to promote maximum student learning. As indicated earlier, this effort develops from each teacher's professional judgment as to the readiness of his or her students to assume new levels of learning and skill development. Too often teachers underestimate their students' ability or willingness to accept higher levels of challenge and responsibility. When this attitude prevails, it can discourage students from meeting their potential as learners of important skills and content. Furthermore, it can cause students to become discontented and bored, or even worse, unaware that their learning ability is being stifled.

In Chapter Seven, we offer tools and guidance for assessing the readiness of students to participate in the various levels of inquiry/discovery instruction. Decisions related to student readiness are based both on aptitude and past experiences. If students seem insecure in taking on new inquiry/discovery responsibilities, it would be wise to begin instruction at Level 1 or Level 2 and gradually introduce them to the next level. In a class of students who vary greatly in their level of inquiry/discovery experience, the less secure students can work in small groups or teams with the more secure students supporting them. There is benefit to both types of students joining together in this "team approach." Students can and do learn from and support each other.

An Inquiry/Discovery Success Story

As we've noted, the inquiry/discovery approach is effective both for teaching science content and developing inquiry "process" skills called for in the National Science Education Standards. By making lessons more varied and interesting, the approach is especially motivating to students who will perform at or above grade level. The approach also can be motivational to students who function below grade level, especially when basic skills learning, along with science, is a primary objective. Such learning is often an objective in instruction targeted for special needs students, or for students who are classified as English language learners (ELLs). In Chapter Six, we highlight some effective strategies for teaching special needs students. Here we present a true "success story" about a large group of sixth-grade ELL students who participated in a special program of inquiry/discovery-oriented instruction in Lancaster County, Pennsylvania, in the mid-1990s. The experimental program, which was initiated by the MERIT Center, involved about twenty teachers and four hundred bilingual students whose primary language was Spanish or Haitian Creole. For the most part, the students were taught in bilingual, "self-contained" classrooms. The ultimate goal of the project was to determine if the ELL students' English-language speaking and writing skills as well as their science learning could be enhanced by involving them in hands-on science experiences. Although the teachers involved in this project had little to no experience with hands-on science instruction, they all agreed to join with two university-level science teacher educators and one ELL specialist in designing and teaching a science-driven English-language curriculum. The teaching was designed to eventually reach Level 1 or above as described by the Instructional Matrix.

In planning their first introductory science unit, which was on meteorology, the teachers initially believed it would be necessary for their students to first memorize definitions for the new scientific terms in English (such as *temperature, pressure, states of matter,* and so on). The "language memorization strategy," they argued, was essential, because many of the students knew little to no English, much less scientific English. In response, the university training team explained that lecturing to students in English, or even having them orally define scientific terms in English, had been proven in previous experience to be ineffective in teaching the meaning of scientific terms, even to regular English-speaking students. In addition, they explained that the "lecture first approach" would not enable students to become involved effectively in inquiry/discovery learning experiences. Even so, the bilingual teachers remained very skeptical.

At this point, the faculty trainers introduced the teachers to the Levels of Inquiry/Discovery Instructional Matrix, and explained how it could be used to structure inquiry/discovery experiences gradually, in steps or levels. The teachers had assumed that hands-on science instruction was an "all or nothing" process. With this new understanding, the teachers agreed to use the Instructional Matrix as the basis for planning instruction, and provided opportunities for students to gradually take on new levels of challenge, both in their hands-on science learning and their English-language development. As an additional benefit, the meteorology unit was designed to include math activities that enabled the students to develop mathematics skills in order to better understand the science content.

With support from the university trainers, the teachers completely rethought and redesigned their approach to both science and English-language instruction, including their use of instructional materials, so that by the middle of the first year of this project the students had advanced from Level 0 to Level 1 in inquiry/discovery learning. A few of the classes had even begun to experience Level 2 instruction, following the Instructional Matrix. By completion of this first school year, not only did the ELL students' test scores indicate that they had learned significantly more science content than had the comparable "control students" in totally English-speaking classrooms (in which the students had been taught science didactically at Level 0), they also exceeded the performance of the "control students" in development of verbal and written English language. And the students performed equally well in mathematics skill development, when compared with the English-speaking control group. By the end of the year, the ELL students were well prepared to participate in instruction at Level 2, to be introduced in their seventh-grade class the following year. Obviously, these encouraging results "sold" the bilingual teachers on the inquiry/discovery approach (Sutman and others, 1997). The reported positive results have also been verified by similar research projects conducted in a number of other school districts.

Summary

The lesson here is that more effective science learning occurs when students of varied cultural and academic backgrounds are engaged in well-designed inquiry/discovery experiences that call upon increasing levels of process skills driven by hands-on investigations. Careful planning will be essential for teachers who are engaging in this instructional approach for the first time and should emphasize ample opportunities for students to be involved in the gradual development of inquiry/discovery skills. The Inquiry/Discovery Instructional Matrix and the Planning Rubric are two tools that teachers can depend on to assist in structuring lesson sequences, or larger lesson units, that effectively promote both skill-building and content learning. With practice and support, and with sensitivity to the students' responses to this different instructional approach, it will be easier to design appropriate lesson experiences that result in students' meeting desired goals in both content knowledge and inquiry learning. It should be mentioned that inquiry/discovery instruction does not need to occur with each and every science lesson. However, the more it can be incorporated when introducing major new science concepts, the more likely students are to develop greater interest in the content and pursue a deeper and more lasting understanding of the concepts.

Chapter 4

Inquiry/Discovery Lessons for Middle School

ON JULY 1, 2005, the American Association for the Advancement of Science (AAAS) published the 125th anniversary issue of its journal, *Science*, which featured a special section, "What We Don't Know" (pp. 75–102). The first article in this section was titled "In Praise of Hard Questions" and was authored by Tom Siegfried. Siegfried opened the article with a quotation from the former nineteenth-century Supreme Court Justice Oliver Wendell Holmes, who once suggested that "great cases make bad laws, however, great questions often make very good science." Siegfried went on to note that, "It is these great questions or inquiries (by students) that provide science, outside and inside the classroom, with motivation and direction."

Middle school students are usually more than ready to ask "hard" or "great" questions if given the opportunity and support by their teachers. In this chapter, we present case examples of three different science lessons, each of which offered students opportunities both to ask leading questions and to search for and discover answers to their inquiries.

At first reading, the content of the lessons may appear to some teachers to be too challenging for middle school students. However, teachers who have taught these lessons in both urban and suburban school environments have judged them to be effective and appropriate for students at these grade levels. The lessons also align well with the inquiry standards for the middle school level proposed by the National Research Council in its publication *Inquiry and the National Science Education Standards* (2000).

National Inquiry Standards: For grades 5 through 8, the fundamental abilities necessary to do scientific inquiry include the following:

- Identify questions that can be answered through scientific investigations.

- Design and conduct a scientific investigation.

- Use appropriate tools and techniques to gather, analyze, and interpret data.

- Develop descriptions, explanations, predictions, and models using evidence.

- Think critically and logically to make the relationships between evidence and explanations.

- Recognize and analyze alternative explanations and predictions.

- Communicate scientific procedures and explanations.

- Use mathematics in all aspects of inquiry.

As readers examine the following case histories of science lessons, the authors encourage them to think seriously about the difference between *meeting* these standards and *addressing* them, perhaps reflecting on your own instruction. Some standards are easily met whereas others are met only through continued practice. Keep in mind that the content area of science that is addressed in each case history, though important, is not the primary determinant for including the lesson here. Our purpose is to show the scope and variety of inquiry/discovery practices that can be introduced in middle school classrooms.

Lesson 1: Astronomy (Measuring Distances)

In his planning, this upper middle school teacher considered introducing the unit on astronomy through a series of lectures to inform students about the history of astronomy developed by ancient Mesopotamian, Egyptian, and Greek mathematicians. On second thought, he hesitated to use this approach, because the science textbook did not include any reference to this history. In addition, it would have meant considerable time spent lecturing to his students about the history of science. At the same time, he learned from the language teacher that these same students recently had focused on ancient Greek culture as they read Homer's *Iliad* and *Odyssey*. Because he was familiar with these Greek classics, he thought of the possibility of beginning the unit with the following quotation from the *Iliad:* "the Bear that turns about a fixed point and is never plunged into the wash of the ocean." He rephrased this classical, poetic description to the following scientific description: "The Big Dipper is a circumpolar constellation of fixed stars that can be seen throughout the night, in our northern hemisphere. And its apparent motion results from the Earth's rotation. While these stars appear to be fixed in relation to each other, they, in fact, are moving rapidly apart in the expanding universe. Even today, in spite of the understanding that the Earth rotates on its axis and that it revolves about the Sun, for the convenience of viewers, we continue to refer to the night sky as if it and its 'inhabitants' move about the Earth.'' This comparison of explanations, he thought, would be a poetic and historically exciting way to begin. But where to head next?

This teacher then reflected on an extended professional development experience that had involved the teachers in a relatively simple activity that enabled them to determine the distance from the Earth to the Sun. Building on that idea, he conceived a unit of study that would involve students in a similar investigation. After consulting with a colleague in the Math Department, who confirmed that the students had completed a course in Euclidian geometry, the teacher designed the unit so that students would have the opportunity to apply one of the basic geometric theorems to a scientific problem, similar to the way that the ancient Greeks had done.

Student Learning Objectives:

- To gain understanding of astronomical distances and geometric relationships

- To develop skills in making systematic observations and accurate measurements, including analysis and interpretation of simple mathematical data

- To develop skills in constructing and using appropriate tools and techniques for collecting, summarizing, and displaying data

- To learn about the importance of historical perspectives in the study of science

Pre-Laboratory Phase

Inquiry

The teacher began the unit by indicating to the students that they might be able to determine the distance from the Earth to the Sun. He then offered the class an opportunity to develop written questions concerning this possibility. They included in their inquiries, ''How might we go about doing this?'' ''Will the bright sunlight and heat prevent us from doing this?'' These types of questions are essential to the inquiry phase of instruction. Here are a few more examples of students' inquiries: ''Isn't this distance too difficult to measure?'' ''How can we travel from here to the Sun to do this? Isn't the Sun too hot to approach?'' ''Doesn't this distance change from when the Sun rises to when it sets?'' ''Is it true that this distance is called one astronomical unit?'' and ''I wonder if we can use the geometry that we are learning in Math class to make our measurement?''

The teacher indicated to his students that he was impressed by the quality of their questions, and assured them that they should be able to answer each of these inquiries, as well as additional ones, by carrying out a relatively simple investigation, adding, ''After all, the ancient Greeks discovered how to do it.'' That comment evoked additional student questions about Greek scientists, to which his response was, ''Let's list all of your inquiries on the query board. During and following our investigation, we will assign teams to search for references that are on our resource shelves for answers. Some of you will explore online sources for further information.''

The students' response to the challenge to actually determine the distance from the Earth to the Sun was ''Cool!'' This reaction was heard even more after the teacher indicated he would evaluate or assess their learning by asking them to design a similar procedure for determining the distance from the Earth to the Earth's Moon. Two of the students, influenced by their experiences with Greek poetry in the English class, indicated that they would reread the *Iliad* to find out references to astronomy in the ancient classic.

Method

To carry out the first investigation, the teacher divided the class into groups of four students each and supplied each group with a set of directions to read, discuss, and follow to determine the distance from the Earth to the Sun.

Student Directions

Prepare the measuring instrument by following the diagram shown in Figure 4.1. Replace the cardboard cover at one end of the tube by taping a piece of aluminum foil over the opening. Make a tiny hole at the center of this piece of foil using a straight pin. Make a 3-cm-long scale, dividing it into lines 1 mm apart. Tape this scale on the inside of the tube cover at the opposite end of the tube so that the scale is vertical to an opening 4 cm × 4 cm that you will cut into the tube itself. This opening should be cut about 7 cm from the end of the tube where the scale is placed.

When completed, one student at a time will point the foil end of the tube toward the Sun, look for the Sun's image on the scale at the opposite end of the tube, and determine the length of the diameter of the image.

Each student in a group will use the determined diameter of the image and calculate an average result. Use this information and other measurements, one being the actual diameter of the Sun, obtained from an appropriate source, to calculate the distance from the pinhole (the Earth) to the Sun.

Student Directions *(Continued)*

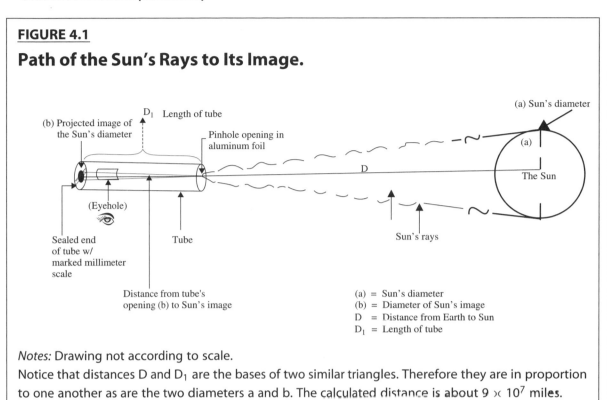

FIGURE 4.1

Path of the Sun's Rays to Its Image.

(a) = Sun's diameter
(b) = Diameter of Sun's image
D = Distance from Earth to Sun
D_1 = Length of tube

Notes: Drawing not according to scale.

Notice that distances D and D_1 are the bases of two similar triangles. Therefore they are in proportion to one another as are the two diameters a and b. The calculated distance is about 9×10^7 miles.

The teacher asked that each group obtain, from home or from a local office supply store, a cardboard mailing tube to be used to create the measuring instrument. He described the tube as being about 65 cm long and 7 to 8 cm in diameter, with at least one end capped by a thin removable plastic cover. In addition to the cardboard tube, the teacher called for each group to supply a piece of aluminum foil measuring about 12 cm square. He said that he would supply the masking tape, scissors, straight pins, metric graph paper with lines marked in millimeters, meter sticks, and Scotch brand tape.

The teacher indicated that each group of students should decide who would be responsible for obtaining the different materials. And each group would read the directions together to determine what to do with these materials. (Wisely, the teacher had extra mailing tubes as backup, should students have been unable to obtain them.)

Once the groups supplied cardboard mailing tubes and other materials, the teacher cautioned the students, several times, never to look directly at the Sun, and to further reinforce this safety requirement, he instructed that each student bring a pair of sunglasses to wear during class the day when the groups would be collecting their data, a day when the Sun would be shining.

The teacher said, "For out-of-school work tonight, it is important that each of you again review the written directions that I've supplied, and begin to interpret the diagram. Then come to class tomorrow with any further inquiries that you have about the procedure." Each student was once again instructed to come to class on the next sunny day with sunglasses to protect his or her eyes. Needless to say, when the students wore sunglasses to school, there were many questions asked by schoolmates about what was happening in the science class.

The next day very few procedural questions were asked. The ones that were asked were addressed and responded to by classmates who had carefully reread and understood their copies of the instructions. Once each group had constructed the measuring tube to be used in the investigation, the students went out into the schoolyard to carry out the procedure.

Laboratory Phase

On this day, the Sun was reasonably high in the morning sky. Students, carrying their observation tubes and wearing their sunglasses, "progressed" to the assigned area for the viewings. (Other students throughout the school continued to inquire about what the class was investigating. Just think of the enthusiasm for science class this simple but dramatic investigative activity generated!) In the schoolyard, the teacher was pleased to hear group members reminding each other not to look directly at the Sun and to keep their sunglasses on.

To obtain the Sun's image, one student from each group pointed the end of the measuring tube, opposite the end with the viewing screen (which was covered with aluminum foil with a pinhole in its center), toward the Sun. By peering into the 4 cm × 4 cm rectangular opening students had cut into the side of the cardboard tube closest to the end that contained the millimeter scale, and with some support from other students in their groups, they could see the Sun's image on the metric scale. Students in each group supported each other through the sensitive process of "fixing" the Sun. In effect, each student had a turn to look through the opening on the side of the tube, "search" for the Sun's image, and direct the Sun's image onto the millimeter scale, from which the image's diameter could be determined.

Once the Sun's image was successfully obtained and measured using the millimeter scale, each observer as instructed kept his or her measured diameter to him- or herself so as not to bias the results obtained by other measurers. Eventually all determinations made by each group were recorded in each group member's laboratory investigation notebook.

Post-Laboratory Phase

Back in the classroom, a comparison of results indicated that students had obtained slightly different values for the diameter of the Sun's image. The values obtained ranged from 5 to 8 mm. Although at first each student was quick to claim that he or she had the "right" answer and those who had other values were mistaken, it became clear that the differences in the measurements of the image's diameter resulted from different interpretations, or perhaps different groups used tubes of different lengths. A general comment was made by the teacher reminding students to look for disparities in approaches when differences in outcome occurred. The teacher suggested that each group consider determining an average value for the image's diameter and using this value in the final computation. This provided an opportunity for students to understand that they could compensate for differences in interpretation through the use of a simple statistical procedure.

During the lunch break, students from this class, as well as other students, posed and answered many inquiries about the investigation. Following completion of the procedure and collection of the data, students returned to their science classroom with additional unresolved inquiries of their own. They added these new inquiries to those recorded the day before. And they removed those inquiries for which they had already discovered answers. Some students commented upon the changeable, ongoing nature of "inquiry."

One student volunteered to draw the geometric diagram on the chalkboard so that all of the students could follow the calculation process together. In doing this, the class decided that they needed to know the real diameter of the Sun. Here the teacher offered support, saying that doing this measurement was beyond the class's scope because of a lack of knowledge of trigonometry or appropriate equipment.

The teacher pointed out, however, that as an alternative, students could search for this value from appropriate references. He had several such references available, including the *Observer's Handbook*, published by the Royal Astronomical Society of Canada (2007), and the *Physical Photometric Data Astronomical Almanac* by the National Almanac Office of the U.S. Naval Observatory (2005). Another source that was available was the Web, by searching under the phrase "sun size." He pointed out that it was common in scientific investigations to draw upon information that others had determined to support new conclusions.

One student from each of the groups searched an available reference to find a value for the diameter of the Sun. Once retrieved, they returned to their groups but compared values across groups. All of these values were given in English units of measure and they varied, but only slightly. The differences led to considerable discussion about sunspots, flares, and the degrees of accuracy in measurement. Several students calculated that the recorded differences in diameter were only about 1%. The class agreed to use an average of these different measurements as the value for the Sun's diameter and to convert the diameter of the Sun's image to the English system of measure.

This need led a student to point out that at least they knew not to use different systems of measurement in their calculations, because earlier, the teacher had posted on the query board a newspaper article about a NASA employee who in calculating the path of a planetary probe did not take into account differences in systems of measure, causing the probe to miss its target, the planet Mars. A student had commented, "The target wasn't that easy to miss." The teacher replied, "But only if you are consistent in the system of measurement you use!" The students had a good chuckle about that, except for one realist who inquired, "How much money was wasted on that project?" No one knew the answer. But one student hazarded the guess that "it was a bundle." Another student, known for his patriotism, asked, "Why is metric preferred anyway? Isn't our English system good enough for them?" The teacher asked that this excellent inquiry be noted for later discussion. When the questioner jotted it down on the query board, he starred and circled it as well, guaranteeing it would not be missed later.

At the teacher's request, and with his support, each student converted the calculated final distance into English miles. The teacher explained that astronomers internationally often express the distance from the Earth to the Sun in miles. He made it clear that no matter which units (whether miles or kilometers) students use to express this distance, it remains fairly consistent. And this distance from the Earth to the Sun is commonly referred to by astronomers as "one astronomical unit" or 1 AU. One student went to the computer to search for information about this new unit, the AU. He discovered that the distances to other planets are often expressed in AUs. The value that the class determined for 1 AU, using the equation based on similar triangles, was 9.27 million miles (93×10^6), a value the teacher indicated confirmed the close reliability of measurements made by earlier scientists.

During the instructional period following the science class, the math teacher asked the students to determine the percentage of difference in comparing their results to the average obtained by astronomers. And he requested that the students consider why their data disagreed at all with that of other scientists. This led to a discussion, during mathematics class, about a number of probable causes.

On the third day of this unit in science class, the students reviewed the additional inquiries posted on the board as part of the follow-up discussions. Once it was established that the students understood what they had accomplished, they each created a written report describing the investigation, including the various items that had been considered. Eventually, several students were selected to read their reports orally to the other students in the science class, and the classmates offered several constructive comments. The teacher congratulated the students for their excellent reports with their clear explanations, statements, and conclusions.

During the discussion period, several students asked how the Greek astronomers determined the Sun's diameter and how it would be determined today. Two of those students were selected to refer to the book *The History and Practice of Ancient Astronomy* by J. Evans (1998) or to Websites about the Sun. The book and other references were available on reference shelves in the school library. The students reported the results from the readings to the remainder of the class. In the process, all of the students were introduced to the meanings of several new terms, such as *transit* and *parallax*.

Assessment Task: Distance from Earth to Moon

To assess student understanding gained during this unit of study, as an outgrowth of the investigation the teacher, as promised, asked each student to develop a plan for determining the distance from the Earth to its Moon and to carry out this plan as an out-of-school assignment on the first night that a half-to-a-full moon would become visible. He reminded the students that for this determination, they could look directly at the Moon. He also gave them a clue that the equipment needed to accomplish this measurement was very simple: a meter stick or ruler, a file card with a 1/4-inch or 6-millimeter circular hole punched in its center, and the use of their eyes. Of course, they had to search for an earlier determined diameter of the Moon through a Website or other resource. Students could eventually work together or alone on this assessment assignment using e-mail, telephone, or personal contact. However, each student was responsible to write his or her report independently; and the report was to include an indication of any cooperation if it did occur. The teacher reminded the students that they would experience again how scientists work together, as needed, to come up with solutions to problems and to give due credit to those who cooperated in finding the discovery.

FIGURE 4.2

Determining the Distance from the Earth to the Moon.

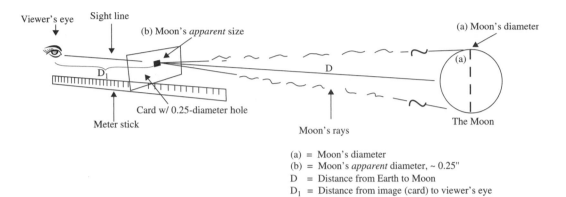

(a) = Moon's diameter
(b) = Moon's *apparent* diameter, ~ 0.25"
D   = Distance from Earth to Moon
D_1 = Distance from image (card) to viewer's eye

Notes: Drawing not according to scale.

Students should be able to notice that by sliding the card back and forth along the meter stick, at some distance from their eye the Moon will appear to fit into the small hole in the card. Once students have searched in references for the diameter of the Moon (a) and have measured the distance from their eye to the card, they will have three of the four values required to calculate the fourth variable, the distance from the hole in the card to the Moon.

$$\frac{\text{Distance from eye to hole}}{\text{(x)Distance from hole to Moon}} = \frac{(1/4'')\text{ diameter of hole}}{\text{Diameter of Moon}}$$

The calculated distance wil turn out to be about 2.4×10^5.

Figure 4.2 is a sample drawing developed by several students who worked together in carrying out this assessment. Every student submitted an appropriate report, either individually or as a member of a group.

In grading these students' reports, the teacher took into account the following components: accurate information, logical deductions, and careful mathematical computations. He also graded for correctly structured sentences, as well as accurate punctuation and spelling. He pointed out that he had served as an editor as part of his role as evaluator. Students were expected to correct grammatical and other mistakes in the same way that scientists would eventually correct their reports before they are placed in a form to be viewed by other scientists.

Extension

A review of the students' reports related to the Earth's Moon led, for example, to the following student inquiries:

1. What causes the phases of the Moon and the tides? Are these related? If so, how?

2. Why does the full Moon appear bigger when it is near the horizon?

3. How long does it take light from the Sun and from the Moon to reach Earth?

4. Why do we only see one "face" or side of the Moon?

Exploring these phenomena generated many additional inquiries by the students, and they were guided to seek answers to each question through appropriate Websites using phrases such as "moon size," "sun size," and "science online," as well as through hardcopy sources (referred to earlier) and NASA's Website.

The students were so interested in this area of study they wanted to learn how these facts were discovered. For this information, students referred, for example, to "Facts on File" at www.factsonfile.com/newfacts. Students with continuing reading difficulties were referred to Websites with pictures maintained by NASA and the National Science Teachers Association (nsta.org). The language used in presentations at these Websites is at manageable readability levels for slower readers. One of the better readers searched and found the article "Is It Time to Shoot for the Sun," a special-focus report that appeared in the July 22, 2005, issue of the journal *Science*. The teacher indicated that this article also would be an appropriate resource to reference for the next unit of study, "Man's Sources of Energy."

As students read and reported information, the following two especially interesting understandings emerged that related to the nature of the scientific enterprise:

1. The dependence of astronomical understanding on mathematics (particularly geometry) was so great that mathematics was considered, historically, to be a science in itself.

2. Egyptian and Greek educated citizens of 2,500 years ago understood that the Earth was spherical instead of flat. Columbus's contribution in the late 1400s was the practical demonstration of validity of this understanding; he used it to attempt to reach India by traveling west across the Atlantic Ocean. Thus he sought to verify empirical knowledge that was assumed to be correct about the shape of the Earth. His efforts demonstrated the discovery portion of a long inquiry/discovery process.

Especially pertinent to sociopolitical issues of today was the discovery by a student who read the *Science* article "Greek Astronomy and the Medieval Arabic Tradition" (July-August 2002). This student reported that during the Dark Ages in Europe, Moslem mathematicians transmitted known mathematical procedures, and some that they themselves invented, to Western European mathematicians and scientists who practiced during the period of the Renaissance. Another student in this class noted the article "Celestial Sightings" (Benson, 2003). He reported, from this article, on recent information discovered by astronomers related to moons revolving about other planets in our solar system, pointing out that the information came from NASA's "Planetary Photojournal" Website (http://photojournal.jpl.nasa.gov) and Michael Benson's book *Beyond: Visions of the Interplanetary Probes* (2003).

The final student observation related to this study was made by the earlier patriotic and doubting student, who now commented, "You are right, the metric system, based on units of 10, is easier to use, but couldn't we rename it something better like the American system?" The class as a whole agreed it had been much more complex to solve problems using English units such as miles rather than metric meters or kilometers.

Comments on Lesson 1 (Astronomy)

Although the students gained important content knowledge through their experience in this astronomy unit, their involvement in hands-on inquiry/discovery practices may have been even more significant and rewarding. By the teacher's structuring the lesson sequence so that the students were responsible for carrying out major tasks, the students were able to gain practice in developing key skills called for in the Science Education Standards. Note by examining Figure 4.1 that students, for example, restructured broad and ill-defined questions, identified inquiries about scientific ideas that could be responded to through relatively uncomplicated mathematical strategies, made reasonably accurate measurements, and designed and executed a simple investigation. They also learned to use appropriate tools and techniques, to base their explanations on observations, to communicate scientific procedures verbally and in written form, and to work with others in designing appropriate procedures and in reporting results. Aside from the merits of this lesson as an inquiry/discovery experience, it is also notable for having enabled students to investigate historical perspectives related to the topic. Such activities make lessons more enriching and also enable students to learn how science is an unfolding endeavor built upon previous discoveries.

In analyzing the "rigor" of this lesson, we note that although the *teacher* decided on the topic to be explored and planned the initial procedure to be followed, the students carried out the procedure (with some guidance) and were responsible for major tasks, including performing the calculations, analyzing the collected data, and determining the distance from the Earth to the Sun. But in some instances teacher support was required. Even so,

TABLE 4.1

Teacher and Student Roles in Astronomy Investigation: A Summary.

Teacher's Responsibilities	Students' Responsibilities
Introduce problem to be investigated. Provide written references and Website access for students to consult.	Develop written inquiries about approaching the problem.
Provide written procedure, most supplies, and safety directions.	Design and construct observation tubes for examining the Sun's image.
Support students in conducting the investigation.	Observe and record the data and compare the results for use in determining average value for the Sun's diameter.
Refer students to investigation diagram.	Determine mathematical relationships for calculating distances.
Provide geometric references.	Determine unknown value in the equations.
Compare results to other scientific findings as a reliability check.	Gather and translate data into measurements (proportions) that can be demonstrated.
	Construct proportional diagrams of other planets and their distances to the Sun.

discussion and follow-up activities emanated from the students themselves. The instruction comes close to being Level 3 based on the Instructional Matrix. Even more interesting, even unique, about this lesson sequence is that the teacher involved the students in a somewhat parallel investigation as both a learning and an assessment strategy. This practice represents the ideal approach to assessment of student learning of both content and process skills development. No direct questions were asked by the teacher. Instead, assessment was based on students' abilities to use gained knowledge to perform effectively in addressing and perhaps meeting the goals stated earlier in the lesson.

Finally, does this lesson, and others like it, allow for *too much* investigating by students? Or, when is enough, enough? The answer to this question lies in both teacher and students recognizing that skill in investigative strategies today is a *must*, especially with available access to the Internet and to the massive amount of hardcopy resources. Although curriculum coverage may have to be curtailed somewhat, enabling students to become involved in such research activities is even more essential if we are to keep them curious and engaged. It is in this way that students will become encouraged to continue in their studies so they can contribute to scientific knowledge, either directly as scientists or indirectly as supportive citizens.

Lesson 2: Study of Mass, Volume, and Density

The following lesson makes use of an investigative activity involving water and ice and enables students to gain an understanding of how density is related to the mass and volume of an object and how this must be considered in comparing the density of two or more objects.

Student Learning Objectives:

- To understand the meaning of mass, volume, and density
- To learn how to accurately compare the density of two or more objects by taking into account mass and volume
- To acquire skills in measuring mass and volume using the metric system

Materials: Each group of four students was supplied with a one-liter plastic soda or water bottle, a source of water, a one-liter plastic graduated cylinder, a metric ruler, a metric balance, and masking tape. A freezer was supplied for all groups of students to use.

Pre-Laboratory Phase

Method: The students were given the procedure as follows: to determine the mass of 1 cubic centimeter (cm^3) of *water* and the mass of 1 (cm^3) of *ice* formed from the water. Half of the groups were directed to use $250\,cm^3$ of water while the other half were to use $500\,cm^3$ of water. Each student was to write in his or her laboratory notebook the procedure that the group designed to carry out the investigation and to record all of the observations, calculations, and conclusions. The teacher instructed them to first determine the density of water followed by determining the density of the ice that forms.

Laboratory Phase

Not knowing the definition for *density*, a student from each group went to the Internet to find it. It of course turned out to be mass/volume. (Students were already familiar with metric units of volume and mass and had used the balance and graduated cylinder in certain investigations.)

The teacher moved from group to group as the students conducted their investigation. Students asked a number of questions, including "Will we obtain different values depending upon which volume of water we begin with?" "Do we take into account the mass of the plastic bottle?" "We obtained a mass of 252.3 g for the water, is this correct?" "Why does the ice occupy more space than the water from which it formed?" "Will the ice have a greater mass?" The only question that the teacher responded directly to was a procedural question: "Do you want to determine the density of just the water or the water plus the bottle?" The answer given was, just the water. Even with this response, several groups forgot to subtract the mass of the plastic bottle in their calculations.

Eventually, each group of students obtained the measurements and determined the density of water; and in comparing results across groups, the students discovered that no matter the volume of water used, the density remained virtually the same. That value was determined to be close to 1. Students had to be reminded by the teacher to add the units of measure ($1\,\text{g/cm}^3$) to this number. Some student groups, using handheld calculators, carried the value for the density of the water to four or five significant figures. And these results led to a discussion, across the class, about "degree of accuracy." In addition, the students generally were amazed at the results. The value they obtained was so close to, if not exactly, $1\,\text{g/cm}^3$!

The teacher then suggested that another group member search the Web for the meaning of the term *specific gravity*. The student determined that the specific gravity of a substance is the comparison of the density of the substance to that of water, used as a standard against which to compare the densities of other substances. This led to the understanding that the value of $1\,\text{g/cm}^3$ is an assigned value that serves as the standard for densities of other substances. The teacher did supply one piece of information. She informed students that the word *specific* used in a description indicates that the property being measured is compared to another standard such as water.

Once the investigation regarding the density of water was completed, the teacher suggested that the students place a strip of masking tape on the outside of the plastic bottle to mark the level of the water's surface, followed by placing the bottle of water in the freezer. Students observed, from time to time, the formation of ice from the surface downward. Once the ice totally formed, the students noticed, somewhat surprised, that the ice occupied more space than had the water. (The level of the surface of ice was above that of the water.) Some students wanted to determine the mass of the ice while other students assured them that the mass was the same as that of the water from which it formed. This difference in perception produced discussion, with the teacher suggesting the students suspend judgment on this difference in perception until the determination of the mass of the ice was completed.

Then the question arose, "How can we determine the volume of the ice?" The members of each group were left to figure this out on their own, only to be reminded by the teacher that they had marked the surface level of the volume occupied by the water with a piece of masking tape. Enough creative students figured out two ways to accomplish this volume determination: (1) Mark the height of the ice's surface with masking tape and then use a ruler to compare the heights of the water and ice. Then by setting up a simple proportion determine the volume of the ice. (2) Allow the ice to melt after its level is marked, followed by filling the bottle with water to the new level and pouring this water into the graduated cylinder. Finally the students determined the density of the ice to be close to $0.94 \, \text{g/cm}^3$. They were surprised to discover that "the ice and water had the same mass" and "Oh! The density of ice is less than the density of water, that's why ice floats on water!"

It was particularly rewarding that the students, in determining this measurement, took into account the principle of accuracy. The teacher then called for each group to write three to five inquiries related to this investigation.

Post-Laboratory Phase

On day three, as students finalized their reports, a number of inquiries were raised about how to design investigations that could be used to determine the densities of a metal, such as steel, and of wood, and of gases, such as air. The teacher indicated that in a few weeks the class would have an opportunity to explore the densities of solids and some gaseous substances. The study of gaseous substances would lead to a unit of study related to how learning about the properties of gases led scientists to understand a number of basic principles of chemistry. The teacher added the students' inquiries about the densities of gases and solids to the list of "future inquiries" posted on the query board, so that they would not be forgotten.

On day four, the teacher requested that each student write a summary of what she or he had learned during this lesson sequence, and to indicate any further inquiries. As an out-of-school assignment, the teacher asked each student to once again look up the term *specific gravity* in the index to their textbook and to be certain they understand the meaning of this term, because it is often used. Also, students were asked to solve six related math problems at the end of the textbook chapter.

Extension: Customarily at the end of each unit or lesson sequence, the teacher asked students to report orally about articles and Website information related to the topic being studied as a way of linking students' investigative findings to historical as well as more recent science and technology understandings. Opportunity for this reporting was rotated to different students. More and more students volunteered to take on this responsibility as the academic year progressed. Students were also encouraged to watch appropriate TV programs on the Science TV channel and to engage their parents as well.

To follow up on the "water and ice" investigation, the teacher asked if a few students would volunteer to pursue related assignments and report back to the class. Two students volunteered to read the article "Water and Ice" from the August 7, 2002, issue of the journal *Science*. In their report, the students talked about how the article presented a thermodynamic and molecular explanation for the many states of water (beyond the two they had just explored). A third student read an article about the unusual behavior of water in the reduced gravity of outer space. He reported on these properties and referred other interested students to "Saturday Morning Science" by Dr. Tony Phillips at the Science@NASA Website (Phillips, 2007). A fourth student presented an oral report to the class on an article addressing the acute shortage of pure water for one-third of the world's six billion people. Her father had helped in finding this article in a magazine he had saved: the November 1993 issue of *Civilization* (pp. 82-83), published originally by the Library of Congress. The author was Mikhail Gorbachev, former premier of the USSR. A fifth student gave a final oral report after reading "Water Works: Research Accelerates Advanced Water Treatment Technologies," an article that appeared in the April 7, 2001, issue of *Chemical and Engineering News*. This article was supplied by the teacher.

Comments on Lesson 2 (Study of Mass, Volume and Density)

In reviewing the teaching strategies emphasized in this lesson, we note that the teacher supported students, as needed, in refocusing poorly stated questions. The group work, with support from the teacher, offered students opportunities to clarify their sometimes incorrect ideas, especially their inquiries about how to proceed. Students were given full responsibility for conducting the investigation, including opportunities to develop their own strategies for solving problems involving quantitative relationships. The students also cooperated in designing one segment of the procedure. Students made a number of measurements and considered the accuracy of these. Appropriate tools were used (balance, graduated cylinder, and so on) and the computer was used to investigate, as well as the handheld calculator. In making comparisons, students discovered that no matter how much water was measured, its density remained the same. The assigned readings led to discussions of alternative sources of pure water and the unusual behaviors of water in an environment other than that at the Earth's surface. Communications, both oral and written, were clearly emphasized. Although descriptions predominated, explanations were not slighted. Alternative explanations were not considered during this investigation, but they were considered in the orally presented report on bonding in water. Students also developed written records of the procedure as well as of the results obtained.

Examining the instructional level of this lesson, it is clear that the students were given the responsibility to carry out the procedures and to collect and analyze the data from their own observations. Students also supplied answers and conclusions related to the original inquiry. Finally, the students took a major role, with some teacher support, in considering how answers or conclusions can be applied or can lead to other inquiries. We can therefore conclude that this lesson is close to a Level 3 presentation according to the Instructional Matrix. One final, but significant observation is that although the content and approach may at first appear to be somewhat challenging for middle school students, recent informal research by the authors indicates that such students, who have experience with this approach, are able to respond favorably to this level of rigor.

Lesson 3: Energy Conservation

The following is a case history describing how a science teacher and a language arts teacher cooperated in introducing a unit called "Energy Conservation." The science teacher had been seeking ways to strengthen students' reading and language skills in order to help them better understand the instructions for conducting science investigations as well as the concepts being taught. The lesson involved three separate investigations.

Pre-Laboratory Phase

To begin, the language arts teacher volunteered to review the "energy kit" (*The Best of Edison Science Teaching Kit*, n.d.), the curricular unit the science teacher had planned to follow with his students. Upon reviewing the kit, the language arts teacher concluded that the students would be able to successfully follow the directions with the science teacher's support, and explained how she would complement the instruction by involving students in language-related activities addressing the topic of energy conservation. The students were informed that the Energy Conservation unit would become part of both their science and language arts instruction. As will be seen, the woodshop teacher was also called on to help.

Student Learning Objectives:

- To develop understanding of how heat energy is used and how this can be measured

- To develop understanding of how and why heat energy can dissipate

- To understand the difference between *temperature* (usually expressed in *degrees*) and *total heat energy* (usually expressed in *calories*)

- To develop understanding of the need for energy conservation practices, and for reducing dependence on energy fuel resources

Laboratory Phase

Investigation (1): Cooling Curves

The science teacher indicated that this first investigation would involve groups of students each placing a glass of water, the temperature of which they would determine, in a portable refrigerator. Each glass of water with its thermometer would remain in the refrigerator over a period of twenty minutes, interrupted every four minutes for a reading of the temperature to determine if any changes in temperatures had occurred. The students noticed that the water's temperature dropped somewhat during each four-minute interval. After the twenty minutes, with all six temperatures recorded (including the initial reading), each group refilled the glass with fresh water and recorded its initial temperature. This time, each glass of water was placed in a small cardboard box, and the glass was surrounded by cotton balls, or strips of cotton. The temperatures were then again recorded. This time the students noticed only slight gradual drops in temperature. Each group of students then decided on three questions or inquiries about this observation and wrote these down for future reference.

Examples of these written inquiries included "Why did the water temperature drop at different rates?" "Did the cotton not allow the cold to pass through the glass into the water?" "What would have happened if we started with water at a higher temperature?" "Would placing tape on the glass produce different results?" "Does the 'color' of the cotton have an impact on the cooling?" "Would the results be similar if we had initially placed ice in the glass?"

The directions for this investigation then directed the students to plot a "cooling curve" for each situation and to determine the average rate of cooling across the groups. The students had some difficulty with this language, so the language teacher helped by rephrasing the directions. ("On a sheet of graph paper, mark down the time intervals 0, 4, 8, 12, 16, 20 minutes along the horizontal or base of the graph paper and the temperatures along the vertical left-hand side of the graph paper.") The science teacher had to explain the following directions: "Calculate and compare the rate of change in temperatures occurring over the twenty-minute period. Calculate the average drop in temperature. Compare the two values and explain any differences."

Investigation (2): Preparing and Using a "Draftometer"

While waiting for the cooling to take place (see previous investigation), each student was given a sheet of directions for constructing a "draftometer" (Figure 4.3). The language teacher supported the students in interpreting the directions for this construction. Eventually, each student proceeded to construct a draftometer in the woodshop, with support from the shop teacher.

The draftometer was made by drilling a quarter-inch hole near the end or top edge of a piece of wood one inch by two inches by ten inches long. A piece of quarter-inch-diameter dowel was glued into this hole. A second piece of wood one inch by two inches by ten inches was glued to the back of the first piece of wood to give additional support. When the draftometer was used, a neatly cut strip of plastic food wrap, five inches by ten inches, was carefully wrapped around the wood dowel. The strip was wound around the dowel until only four inches of it flapped freely. Three thumbtacks were used to hold this plastic strip to the dowel. Students took this draftometer home to check for drafts of cold air around windows and doors. (See Figure 4.4.)

During a later science and English class period, students developed written inquiries about the causes for drafts in their homes and indicated how these causes could be lessened—and more important, why they should be lessened. The English teacher helped the students to construct a carefully worded letter to parents about the need for checking on drafts and how drafts increase the use of fuel and fuel costs.

FIGURE 4.3

Constructing a Draftometer.

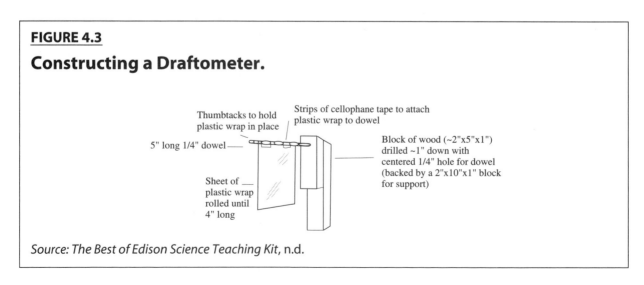

Source: The Best of Edison Science Teaching Kit, n.d.

FIGURE 4.4

Using a Draftometer.

Investigation (3): Temperature versus Heat Content

The science teacher explained to his language colleague that their students would be assigned to complete this investigation both at school and at home, just like the earlier investigation. It would extend the message of fuel efficiency and teach students, through actual experience, the difference between temperature and heat content.

Students, whose homes had bathtubs with both a drain control and a shower, were assigned to collect the data related to this investigation. Each student was assigned to take a traditional bath using the tub and to measure and record the volume of water used, as well as the temperature of the water at the beginning of the bath. The next time they were to bathe, these same students were directed to take a shower and to allow the water to collect in the tub. They were then to measure and record both the volume of the water and its temperature. In addition, the temperature of the bathroom was also to be recorded. To collect the data, the teacher supplied each student with a kit containing a metric ruler (for measuring the volume of water) and a centigrade or Celsius thermometer (for measuring the temperature of both the water and the room). Eventually, the students presented their data to the class, with the volume of water identified in cm^3 and the temperatures in ^oC.

In analyzing the data collected, the class learned that their showers generally used a smaller volume of water than did their tub baths. Through this investigation, the students also learned to distinguish between temperature (as measured in degrees) and total heat content (measured in calories). The students came to understand these differences by calculating the *calories* of heat that were required to raise the temperature of the water from "room temperature" to the warmer "bathing temperature" required for a bath or shower. This same data was used in an activity later in the unit, in which students calculated the cost of electricity required to produce a given number of calories of hot water.

The science class spent two weeks of instruction considering the many sources used to supply heat energy for a single family per week, and then for the nation as a whole for the same amount of time. Appropriate Websites were referred to in order to learn more about the use of coal, oil, natural gas, nuclear fuel, solar radiation, agricultural products, hydrogen fuel cells, and wind and waves as sources of energy to produce heat and also electricity. The class also compared the efficiencies of different technologies in producing light energy as well as the mechanical energy required to "run" automobiles. In this and in follow-up investigations, students were introduced to new terms and phrases related to energy use and were able to gain a limited understanding of their meanings, including, for example, *changes in forms of energy, molecular motion, specific heat, heat of fusion, heat of vaporization, energy cell,* and so on.

Language Contribution: During the two weeks devoted to this science unit, the English teacher involved these same "science" students in searching the Web and other sources for key words and definitions associated with energy and its applications to human activity. As a closing assignment, she asked each student to write an original essay that emphasized the significance of energy sources to them personally and to the future well being of the nation. The written reports were posted on the hallway bulletin board. Two of the reports were selected for the school's monthly newspaper: Several students asked to learn more about the inventor-scientists Thomas Edison and his African American associate Howard Latimer. Information about these men as well as other scientists was found in *The Best of Edison Science Teaching Kit*, referred to earlier.

Comments on Lesson 3 (Energy Conservation)

Both teachers were gratified by the enthusiasm and success students experienced during the teaching of this lesson sequence. Students proved to be engaged successfully in this instruction, to the degree that when they had difficulties with reading materials they generated excellent inquiries and they shared both their inquiries and discoveries with classmates.

In addition, because there were two or even three instructors cooperating in supporting students, the instructors were able to take the necessary time to involve the students in their search for appropriate answers to inquiries. The language teacher was especially pleased with the cooperative experience because of the emphasis on the "constructed response" approach in school district testing. This approach involves students in learning to write about things that are other than literature-based.

Summary

In addition to addressing the standards for middle school science instruction, the instruction described in this chapter addressed specific societal-environment and energy issues and the basic science content understanding required to begin to accurately appreciate and assess the importance of those societal concerns. Even the introductory astronomy lesson sequence made it possible for students to focus on our primary source of energy: the Sun. Although the latter part of the chapter did not include the detail offered in the first part of the chapter concerning investigative procedures in which students can be involved, the information is available through the aforementioned *Best of Edison Science Teaching Kit*. The authors argue that the mix of basic science with its applications is useful especially for middle school–level students. Finally, the description of cooperation among teachers of different disciplines represents a significant approach to extend upon.

Facilitating Inquiry/Discovery Practice

Middle school students generally have less opportunity to practice inquiry/discovery than should be the case. To further facilitate inquiry/discovery practices in these grades, we encourage teachers to divide the class into student teams so that members can assist one another while carrying out investigations and in recording the results. Teams work best when there is the expectation that they themselves should decide how best to work together in carrying out the investigative procedures. Don't be surprised if this team approach does not work well at first. In introducing inquiry/discovery practices, the teacher may initially have to offer more direction. Whatever strategy works best in terms of meeting your goals for students, teachers should avoid excessive "teacher telling."

Teachers can best develop students' self-sufficiency by being persistent in their expectations and by *not* expecting every student to be at the same level of understanding at the same time. This attitude is essential for success in learning. Also, teachers should not expect every student to read the same information or to review the same Website at the same time. Instead, students should be expected to share information with each other, and instructional practices should be designed to support this sharing.

The best role for each teacher to follow is to serve as a source of guidance in the information-gathering process. For example, teachers can direct individual students or groups of students to specific references. Or they may suggest to students having difficulty in finding information, "Why don't you look in the index of our text for ..." or, "Why not have your group make a list on the chalkboard of the words and phrases that have resulted in useful 'hits' for other students to refer to," or, "Share the discovery you just made with your group or with the entire class." One approach that is useful but is seldom heard is, "Mary just taught me (the teacher) something I did not know before about...."

Near the beginning of the school year, the teacher may have to demonstrate how to use a piece of equipment required for carrying out an investigation. If so, follow this demonstration by requesting that a student demonstrate it to the class, under your guidance. Later in the year individual students within each group will be able to take this responsibility as you, the teacher, monitor the process. The teaming by teacher and students together is most productive, in terms of overall learning and attitude development, when the teacher recognizes when to *step in* and when to *step back*. In the mentor role, the teacher provides most, but not all, of the necessary materials and other resources that assist students as they develop the skills associated with the Standards. In summary, the teacher need never to take over the total responsibility for student learning and should never take away students' pride related to areas in which they are achieving or have achieved.

Chapter 5

Inquiry/Discovery Lessons for High School

IN THIS CHAPTER we indicate how science instruction can be designed to offer high school students opportunities to practice ever higher levels of inquiry/discovery. As in the previous chapter we present case histories of lesson sequences that have proven to result in successful content learning and that have also served to motivate students to pursue learning in the sciences. The approach enabled students to effectively address the national standards for skill learning as proposed by the National Research Council in its publication *Inquiry and the National Science Education Standards* (2000). The "inquiry" standards for high school are the ability to

- Identify questions and concepts that guide scientific investigations
- Design and conduct scientific investigations
- Use technology and mathematics to improve investigations and communication
- Formulate and raise scientific explanations and models using logic and evidence
- Recognize and analyze alternative explanations and models
- Communicate and defend scientific arguments

This chapter includes five case histories of lessons that not only address these standards but also include content from three areas of science: physics, chemistry, and biology. The fourth lesson is linked to the earth sciences, and the fifth is interdisciplinary in nature.

Lesson 1: Energy, Work, and Power (Physics)

This lesson introduces understandings upon which a component of physics, "mechanics," is based. It begins with an investigation that enables students to explore the concepts of energy and work. Having learned in earlier grades that any push or pull is a *force,* students recall that simple definition of *force* as they come to understand the meaning of the terms *energy* and *work.* In a subsequent investigation, students learn how these concepts connect to an understanding of physical (*mechanical*) power.

Student Learning Objectives:

- To develop an understanding of how energy, power, and work are related

- To gain understanding of how force and distance can vary in accomplishing work

- To overcome the common misconception that it is possible to reduce the amount of work required to accomplish a given task

- To develop skills in designing investigations, collecting and analyzing scientific data, and formulating conclusions based on data

Lesson 1a: Energy and Work

Inquiry: The teacher did not directly state a problem but instead suggested to students that they would be engaging in an activity connected to a definition for *force.*

Method: To prepare for this investigation, the teacher secured ten pounds of stones placed in a large pail with a handle, heavy-duty scales with a hook that could be used to lift or pull the pail of stones, a ten-foot-long board, a yardstick, and a Magic Marker.

Investigation: The teacher invited a few students to lift the pail of stones and hook it onto the scales. She then invited her class to carry these items outside to the front steps of the school. Two of the students were asked to weigh the pail both with and without the stones. The weight of the pail turned out to be one pound, and the pail and stones together to be eleven pounds. One student was then called on to lift the scales with the pail of stones attached. Reminding students that they already knew that a *force* was required to lift or pull objects, the teacher asked students to notice the amount of force required as the pail was lifted vertically to a height of three feet and to other heights. Observing this, the students quickly noted that the force required was eleven pounds and that this force remained the same no matter how high the pail was lifted. That is, the required lifting force never changed. It remained constant.

The teacher then said, "Let's lift the pail to a three-foot height in two different ways and compare the forces required." One student responded, "Well, we already know that it takes eleven pounds of force to lift the pail directly up. What if we used the scale to drag the pail up an inclined board?" Two students proceeded to lay the board diagonally on the school steps, beginning at ground level with one side of the board near one edge of the steps. Two other students then used the yardstick to mark the board where the height measured three feet from the ground. The teacher now invited students to determine the amount of force that would be required to move the pail up the inclined board to the three-foot high mark. Because it previously took eleven pounds of force to lift the pail vertically, students assumed that the same amount of force would be required to pull it up the incline. To the amazement of most students, the force required turned out to be less than eleven pounds. In fact, it was only seven! One student remarked that the board enabled them to accomplish the goal with four pounds less force, or much less effort, compared with lifting the pail vertically. They also noticed that the student who was applying the force (doing the pulling) could stop to rest without the pail falling to the ground. Following this activity, the teacher invited students to offer inquiries based on their observations. Following are examples of the inquiries:

- Why did it take less force to pull the stones up the ramp to the three-foot-height mark than was required to lift the stones vertically?

- We actually moved the pail up the board a distance of about eight feet in order to lift them three feet from the ground. How do we take this into account?

- Why didn't the pail slide back down the board when we stopped applying the force of seven pounds?

- Wouldn't it have been easier simply to carry the pail of stones up the steps?

The "investigators" returned to the classroom, where their inquiries were posted on the query board to be addressed. The teacher then asked the students to think about what they had just observed, and to do this by drawing a diagram representing the procedure and their observations, in their laboratory notebooks, correctly labeling the diagram. (Figure 5.1 is an example of one student's diagram.)

Conclusions: The teacher divided the class into teams of two or three students and assigned each team to search for definitions of the terms that developed from the students' inquiries: *force, energy, work (physical), effort, weight, friction*, and also *"inclined plane" used as a "simple machine."* Students were referred to both print and computer resources, including the physics textbook, a dictionary, and Websites for conducting their searches, which extended to an out-of-school assignment.

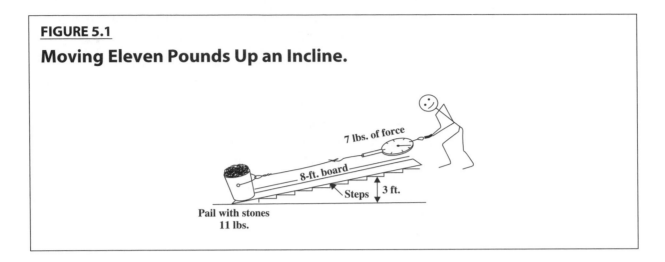

FIGURE 5.1

Moving Eleven Pounds Up an Incline.

During the following class period, the entire class shared their findings with the teacher, who clarified definitions as needed. Each student was then assigned to write in his or her laboratory notebook a summary explanation of their findings. Here is a typical example of such a summary:

Physical work is accomplished by applying a force to an object so that the object moves. The amount of energy required to accomplish this work is determined by the amount of force required times the distance over which the object is moved. This energy is determined by the following formula: w(work) = f(force) × d(distance). Since it requires energy to accomplish physical work, energy is expressed in the same units of measure as work: for example, ft. lbs., g. cm. or other combined units of force and distance.

In our investigation we discovered that 33 ft. lbs. of physical energy were used and 33 ft. lbs. of work was accomplished in lifting the 11 lbs. of stones and pail vertically to a height 3 ft. from the ground. Pulling this same pail of stones up the inclined board required 56 ft. lbs. (8 ft. × 7 lbs.) of energy or work to accomplish the same goal. That is, use of the inclined board meant that we had to use more energy and do more work than had we lifted the stones directly. However, the work was easier to do because it was accomplished with less effort or force (7 lbs. instead of 11 lbs.). We forfeited distance for force. Some of the force required was used to overcome friction between the board and the pail of stones.

Subsequently, the students developed several generalizations from their discoveries resulting from this lesson. Following are some examples:

- The force required to lift an object is determined by the need to overcome Earth's gravitational pull toward its center. Moving an object at an angle other than 180° from a line drawn from the object to be moved to the Earth's center requires a reduced force but at the expense of distance.

- Friction exists between objects being moved over surfaces. This friction is overcome by applying additional force. The friction also prevents the object to be moved from sliding back.

- Pulling the pail up the slanted board served as a type of "simple machine": inclined plane, wheel and axle, and pulley and lever. Simple machines can be combined to form more complex machines that also reduce the effort or force required to accomplish work, but at a price. That price is having to move the force over a greater distance than would be required without the machine or without having to overcome friction.

During the summary, one student team inquired, "Is the time that it takes to accomplish work ever considered in accomplishing work?" The teacher responded, "In fact, your inquiry leads to the topic of our next lesson: the meaning of physical or mechanical power. For homework, search the Web and the textbook for a definition(s) for *power*, and we will consider your findings during the next investigation."

Lesson 1b: Study of Mechanical Power

Method: At the beginning of the next class session, the leader of the student team that posed the inquiry about the role that time plays in accomplishing work (or in "using" energy to accomplish work) reported the team's findings to the class. Their report indicated that "physical or mechanical power," according to a Website on the subject, is simply defined as "work accomplished over a given period of time." The team interpreted this, correctly, to also mean *energy expended over time*. The example given on the Web gave the English units for power: ft. lbs./sec. or ft. lbs./min. It also included the following conversion factor: 1 horsepower or 1 HP = 33,000 ft. lbs./min. or 550 ft. lbs./sec.

With this introduction, the teacher invited the students, with her support, to design an investigation that would enable each student to determine how much power he or she could or would expend in lifting himself or herself from one floor of the school building to the next floor. Through considerable deliberation, the students decided that knowing their own weights, running or walking up a flight of stairs of known height, and determining how long it would take to accomplish that goal, would give them the needed data. Each student would be serving as both the source of the energy *and* the object to be lifted. The students further decided that the following materials would be needed: scales to weigh

TABLE 5.1

Results from the Investigation of Mechanical Power.

Runner	Weight of Runner (in lbs)	Height (in feet)	Work (in ft. lbs)	Time (in sec)	Power (in ft lbs/sec)	Horsepower (H.P.)
1		12				
2		12				
3		12				
4		12				
Etc.						
Example	150	12	1.800	6.0	300	0.55

Note: 1 H.P. = 550 ft lbs/sec

each student, a yardstick, a length of string to measure long distances, stopwatches for determining the time each student takes to go up the flight of stairs, and a calculator. The class agreed to divide into teams, with each team covering a different stairwell between two floors. Each team also created a table for recording the collected data. (See Table 5.1.) Each team further agreed to rotate roles, so that each student had an opportunity to run, keep time, measure distances, and serve as a "guard." The guard was to ensure that students from other classes using the stairs would not become injured by colliding with the physics students.

Investigation: Each team gathered at its assigned stairwell, measured the height to be covered in the "runs," and recorded this on the chart. Each student was then weighed, and this also was recorded. As the investigation proceeded, it turned into a competition for determining who could generate the greatest power output, as each student's run was timed and recorded. After conducting their runs, the teams returned to the classroom and posted their charts.

In reviewing the data, the teacher noted that the recorded height measurements varied from 12.34 feet to 22.5 feet. She concluded that some groups must have measured the distance up the diagonal steps while other groups, *correctly*, measured the vertical height from one floor to the next. The incorrect measurements resulted from groups not remembering that effective work is accomplished by moving each student's weight vertically. Also, measurements in a few instances were carried out to an inappropriate number of significant figures. Everyone agreed that it would be reasonably accurate to round the numbers to the nearest foot (12 ft.); not to the nearest hundredth of a foot. With these changes, each student calculated his or her power output in ft lbs/sec and converted this to horsepower by dividing this value by 550 ft lbs/sec. The calculated values for a student's horsepower ranged from 0.3 to 1.2 H.P.

Conclusions: Rather than summarizing this lesson by lecturing to students about energy existing in various forms, the teacher decided to give students a homework assignment. She reminded students that they had been studying mechanically produced power only as expressed in horsepower units, but that the term *power* could be applied to other forms of energy, such as electrical power, chemical power, and nuclear power. Students were assigned to find units of measure for these other forms of power and also to explain how other forms of energy were "harnessed" and used.

Following this investigation the teacher turned the students' attention to solving six appropriate or related mathematical problems that appeared at the end of the textbook chapter "Energy, Work, and Power."

Comments on Lesson 1 (Energy, Work, and Power)

The first lesson is notable in that the teacher *did not* begin the instruction by defining the unfamiliar terms. Instead she created a need for students to understand the definitions by directly involving them in the "pail lifting" investigation. Not announcing the problem or topic immediately creates opportunities for students to inquire. As the investigation began, students were encouraged to apply their prior understanding of force to a new situation. Numerous inquiries arose during the course of the lesson, most of which were responded to by the students themselves with guidance from the teacher. The summary of Lesson 1a generated yet an additional inquiry that, in turn, served as a lead-in to Lesson 1b. The team report following up on that inquiry provided essential information that enabled the students, at the teacher's invitation, to collectively design an investigation exploring how physical power is expended. Instead of the conventional lecture summary at the end of the lesson, the teacher decided to assign an additional discovery project that required students to learn about related forms of energy and power. The amount of class time required to learn through investigating and searching for answers, of course, was greater than would have been required had the teacher simply defined terms and solved a few mathematical problems. However, experience conducting this lesson indicates that students find the instruction both informative and exciting. Students outside the class who happen upon the activities in the stairwells and hallways are often overheard saying, "Hey, I want to take that science class next year!"

Lesson 2: Study of Cell Sizes: A Simulation (Biology)

This lesson is of particular significance because more students are enrolled in biology or life science courses in grades 8 through 12 than in any other science discipline. Also, many high school biology textbooks discuss the cell sizes of organisms. However, teachers seldom offer students opportunities to *investigate* cell size in much detail.

Student Learning Objectives:

- To develop understanding of how the dimensions of a cell are related to its survival and well being

- To lay the groundwork for a more detailed study of cell structure and function

- To develop skills in use of mathematics and in the preparation of graphs to support analysis and explanation of scientific findings

Inquiry: In introducing this lesson, the teacher reminded students that earlier they had examined, under the microscope, the cells of the plant Elodea, cells of the root tip of the onion plant, and epithelial cells from the inner lining of their own mouths. She asked the students to consider the sizes of these cells in relation to the size of the total organism. This consideration was followed by a request that each team of three or four students develop in writing inquiries that came to mind as they read the title of the investigation. Each team's inquiries were placed on the query board. Eventually, the discovery related to each of these was written by students and placed on this board next to the original inquiry.

Method: The preceding preliminary activity was followed by the teacher distributing to each student a copy of "Directions for Investigating Cell Size (A Simulation)" (Exhibit 5.1). The teacher also distributed a rubric for evaluating preparation of the graph called for in the instructions, and for assessing other aspects of the student's participation in the investigation (Table 5.2). Each team of students was then asked to review both the directions and the rubric and to raise any concerns that they might have.

Investigation: Following the directions, the student teams constructed four simulated cells of differing sizes by using cardboard. They then measured the total surface of each "cell" and used the data to calculate cell volume, recording the data (length, corresponding area, volume) in a table specifically designed for this purpose. Referring to the data in their table, each student within each team prepared a graph. Each graph was to have two curves, one curve indicating cell volume and the other curve indicating cell surface area, with each curve plotted against the corresponding lengths.

EXHIBIT 5.1

Directions for Investigating Cell Size (A Simulation).

Materials Needed

A pattern for use in constructing simulated cells of different sizes (the simulated cells will be cubes with sides 1, 2, 3, and 4 inches in length constructed from a sheet of cardboard); scissors; glue; a packet of enough dry sand to eventually fill 4 in.^{3} of space; hand calculators; sheets of English measurement-ruled graph paper; English ruler; pencils of two different colors; overhead transparencies of graph paper; an overhead projector; graduated cylinders (probably metric-scaled but preferably English-scaled); and access to the Internet.

Preliminary Procedure

Cut enough cardboard squares of 1, 2, 3, and 4 inches to make a cube of each size (1 in.^{3}, 2 in.^{3}, etc.). Glue these to form cubes but leave one side of each cube open. (These cubes represent cells of different volumes.)

Procedure

1. Determine the total surface *area* of each of these simulated cells, including the open end.
2. Determine the *volume* of each "cell" both mathematically and experimentally. If the graduated cylinder is marked in metric units, convert these to English units. To accomplish this look up the conversion factors in a handbook or appropriate text.
3. Record each length, corresponding area, and volume in a table that you design for this purpose. Appropriately label the columns and the title of this table of simulated data.
4. Design the table of data so that it can include data for six additional "cells" of 5, 6, 7, 8, 9, and 10 inches in length. Don't construct these "cells." Instead, determine the data using the process followed in procedures 1 and 2 above. That is, use the calculations used with the earlier data as a model.
5. Using the graph paper, plot two curves or bar graphs using a different-colored pencil for each graph. The first graph should indicate the volume of each "cell" plotted against the corresponding length of each side. The second graph (plotted on the same sheet of graph paper) should indicate the total surface area of each "cell" plotted against the corresponding length of each side.

Conclusions: Following preparation of the graphs, each team was instructed to select one completed graph and to transpose it onto an overhead transparency for presentation to the class. An example of one team's graph is presented as Figure 5.2. Guided by the teacher, students were asked to examine the graphs to determine the point at which cell volume outpaced the surface area. Comparing the results from team to team, and using the rubrics as a guide, the class was led in discussion of the accuracy of the graphs as well as the significance of the simulated data as it applied to the structure and condition of actual living cells.

Questions posed by the students included "Why do living cells generally have small volumes compared to the total volume of the organisms of which they are a part?" "What factors limit the sizes of living cells?" "How

TABLE 5.2

Rubric for Assessing Results of the Lesson Sequence: Sizes of Cells.

Student's Name:		
Part I Rubric for Report of Investigation		
Category	**Specific Area**	**Assessment**
Neatness and Orderliness of Report	Report of Investigation	YES NO
	Graph	YES NO
	Graph labeled?	YES NO
Completeness of Report	Pre-Laboratory questions answered?	YES NO
	Table of data complete?	YES NO
	Post-Laboratory questions answered?	YES NO
Completeness of Graphs	Graph completed in pen/pencil/colors?	YES NO
	Graph titled?	YES NO
	Graph is effective size?	YES NO
	Graph has legend?	YES NO
	X-axis is labeled?	YES NO
	X-axis shows values?	YES NO
	Y-axis is labeled?	YES NO
	Basic construction or observation made?	YES NO

Part II Rubric for Assessment and Final Grade			
Category	**Specific Activity**	**Points: 8 (maximum)**	**Points: 0 (minimum)**
Data and Related Calculations	Presented in tabular form and labeled		
	Calculations are correct		
Graphic Representation	Title clearly stated		
	X-axis: clear title(s)		
	X-axis: appropriate units spaced correctly		
	Y-axis: clear title(s)		
	Y-axis: appropriate units spaced correctly		
	Curve(s) appropriately developed from data, neatly drawn		
	Legend clearly data presentation—uses color where appropriate		
Questioning and Conclusions	Questions asked are appropriate		
	Responses to questions appropriate		
	Valid conclusions drawn		
	Four additional points for other factors		
Scoring: A = 100 − 90 B = 89 − 80 C = 79 − 70 D = 69 − 60 F = 59 − below	Total Score:		

FIGURE 5.2

Cell Areas and Volumes Plotted Against Corresponding Lengths.

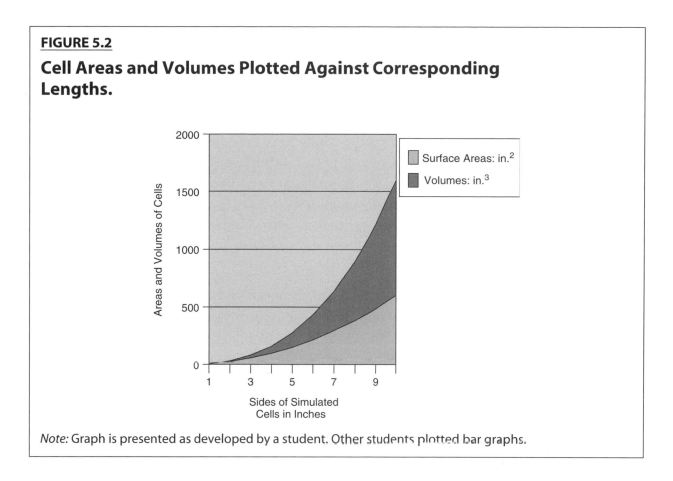

Note: Graph is presented as developed by a student. Other students plotted bar graphs.

large can a cell become and yet remain physically healthy over time?'' ''How do the data we have collected and plotted graphically help us to analyze the effectiveness of cells in transporting nutrients and in carrying out other functions?''

The teacher referred students to a Website to support them in responding to the preceding inquiries. The Website is The Biology Project: ''Cell Biology,'' at www.biology.arizona.edu/cel_bio/tutorials/cells/ cells2.html. Students were also referred to articles such as ''Chemical Biology of the Cell'' by S. Borman (2006) and the introductory article related to cell signaling, ''Size, Mates and Fates,'' by N. Gough (2006). These students reported to the class what they had learned from these readings, generating further inquiries about cell structure, chemical structure of cells, and so on.

Extension: During subsequent class periods, this teacher involved her students in related investigations regarding cell size, including one she discovered in an article from the October 4, 2004, issue of *The Science Teacher*, ''How Small Is a Cell,'' by G. Rau. Following the procedure described in that article enabled students to ''estimate the number of yeast cells in a grain of dry yeast, as well as the number of yeast cells used in making a loaf of bread." (Directions for obtaining this article are available through www.store.nsta.org.)

For the final activity in this lesson sequence, each student was assigned to develop a written response to one of the many inquiries that developed during the investigation. The questions included "Are there any organisms constructed of unusually large cells?" "If so, how do these large cells obtain nutrients and excrete wastes?" "Is there any situation in which a large cell volume compared to cell area might be an advantage?" "How do cells cooperate in sharing control of gene expression in cell division and in facilitating transport of water, minerals, and other substances?"

Comments on Lesson 2 (Study of Cell Sizes)

This lesson shows that effective inquiry/discovery instruction does not always require elaborate laboratory facilities. In this case, simple, hands-on visual materials were used to help students gain understanding of complex scientific processes by inspiring further research and inquiry. The lesson also responds, at a beginning level, to the national appeal among practicing biologists to incorporate the use of mathematical skills and updated content into biology instruction, in order to bring the study of biology in line with the approach practiced by biologists today. Tying biology and mathematics together makes both subjects more meaningful to students. And if teachers of both subjects plan together, instruction can be designed so that students will better appreciate both subjects.

Lesson 3: Effects of Chemicals on Metabolism (Biology and Chemistry)

The following case history describes an investigation that involved students in observing the effects of both ethanol and caffeine on the heartbeat of the water flea, Daphnia. The investigation can be of relevance to students studying either life or chemical sciences.

Student Learning Objectives:

- To develop understanding that certain chemical substances effect the metabolism and behavior of living organisms

- To learn about the structure of a class of living organisms: crustaceans

- To be introduced to applications of science laboratory research related to human health

- To develop skills in the practice of inquiry/discovery

Materials: For each team of two students: a binocular microscope, a depression slide, a single Daphnia, a pipet, a filter or lens paper to use in draining excess water, a small bottle of ethanol solution, a small bottle of coffee solution, and a student-owned watch with sweeping second hand.

Chemical Solutions (prepared by teacher): Alcohol: add $1\,cm^3$ of alcohol to $99\,cm^3$ of water; caffeine: add $1\,cm^3$ of brewed caffeinated coffee to $99\,cm^3$ of water. Place each solution in a small dropper bottle and label.

Inquiry: The teacher began this lesson by introducing students to a crustacean: Daphnia, or "water flea." Students were instructed to search with the term *Daphnia* for Websites until they found a site that described the structure of the organism, in detail, with particular emphasis on its heart muscle. In conducting their search, students learned that the Daphnia heart muscle could be observed beating in a live specimen by using a binocular microscope.

Method: Following the introduction, the teacher demonstrated how to mount a live Daphnia specimen on a depression microscope slide for observation, and how to control its movement by reducing the amount of water surrounding the specimen. He also described how each team of two students could cooperate in counting the rate of the beating heart muscle during a period of fifteen seconds and to convert this value to beats per minute.

The teacher conducted a trial run to ensure that the concentrations were appropriate for the Daphnia. (*Note:* it is best to maintain all solutions and culture water at room temperature because changes in temperature affect the rate of the beating heart muscle.) The teacher also made sure that students knew how to correctly use the binocular scope, and suggested that they conduct a "trial run" before starting the formal investigation.

Investigation: Working in teams of two, one student observed the heart muscle and counted the beats, while the other student kept track of the time period (fifteen seconds) and marked off the counts with a slash mark on a piece of paper. One trial was conducted with the Daphnia in pond or culture water. The pond water was then removed by using the filter or lens paper, and it was quickly replaced with the alcohol solution. Eventually, a third trial was conducted using the caffeine solution. The students rotated roles at each trial, and their results were averaged. The data were then converted to beats per minute, with the data from each team recorded in one master table for the entire class (Table 5.3). All living Daphnia were returned to the culture container.

Conclusions: In reviewing the master chart, the students noted considerable variations in the observed heart muscle beats per minute in the data collected by teams. However, the data clearly indicated that the ethanol

TABLE 5.3

Record of Heart Muscle Beats for Daphnia: Sample Data.

Student Teams	Measured in Pond Water	Measured in 15% Ethanol	Measured in 15% Coffee (caffeine)
1	68	44	76
2	60	40	72
3	64	48	72
4	52	36	68
Etc.			
Average Beats/minute	244	168	288

Note: Data is for 15 seconds. Multiply by 4 for beats/minute.

solution caused the rate to slow down considerably, while the caffeine produced the opposite effect, a considerable increase in rate. This raised a number of student questions, including "Why did these two substances have such an impact on the rate of the beating heart muscle of the Daphnia?" "Why were the effects so different?" "Do these substances have similar impacts on humans?" Considerable discussion also ensued related to the impact of alcohol, caffeine, and other drugs on human metabolism and behavior. To follow up on the inquiries and comments, the teacher assigned students, as homework, to visit the "MadSci Network" Website (www.madsci.org), where they could find much more information about the impact of different substances and conditions on heart rate. Each student was assigned to return to class the next day with one or two new facts that they had discovered in answer to their inquiries through this search.

Access to the information above and experiences led students to inquire further not only about the impact of "drugs" on the metabolism of Daphnia, but also the impact of "entertainment drugs" on humans. For example, students inquired about the relationship of taking such drugs to acquiring HIV-AIDS. To address these more personal questions or inquiries, the teacher referred students to books and magazine articles that he had collected that were pertinent to this critical topic. An example of these references was the popular book *Freakonomics*, by S. D. Lewis and S. J. Dubner (2003). One chapter in that book, "Why Do Drug Dealers Still Live with their Moms?" was of particular interest to the students. Another publication of particular interest was *Science Medicine and Animals: A Circle of Discovery*, by the National Research Council (2005), because it described examples of the value to humans in cautiously using animals in medical research. The examples included the development of antibiotics in treating many bacterial infections as well as reduction in cases of malaria throughout the tropical world. Time was set aside at a later date for these students to report what they had learned from these readings.

Comments on Lesson 3 (Effects of Chemicals on Metabolism)

This lesson is notable in that it offered opportunity for students to conduct an investigation with potential applications to human health. If they are students of biology, they also develop an understanding of crustaceans as a class of organisms. If they are students of chemistry, they learn about the properties of both alcohol and caffeine and their potentially harmful impacts on the metabolism of an organism. In either case, students gain understanding of how a scientific study can have relevance to their personal lives.

Lesson 4: Study of Hydrogen, Oxygen, and Water (Chemistry)

The following lesson sequence was included early on in a high school chemistry course and included three separate lessons. Students were first involved in an investigation exploring the decomposition of water into its two elements: hydrogen and oxygen. This was followed with a demonstration designed to show the recombination of these two elements to produce water. One of the objectives to be met through demonstrating this reverse reaction will become very obvious as you read further. As an additional follow-up, students were engaged in a model-building activity. Once again, notice that the lesson sequence began with an investigation from which definitions and understandings eventually emerged.

Lesson 4a: Decomposition of Water

Student Learning Objectives:

- To build an understanding of the nature of chemistry, especially the chemical concept of oxidation and reduction

- To begin to understand the role of electrical energy in the decomposition (or breakdown) of chemical compounds

- To explore applications of chemistry to today's scientific and industrial world

- To develop skills in performing laboratory practices and in formulating explanations of scientific processes, including the use of visual models

Materials: Student-type Hoffman electrolysis apparatus, a 9- or 12-volt battery as a source of direct electric current (DC) (or use a DC source supplied directly to laboratory tables), water (tap or distilled), dilute sulfuric acid (prepared by the teacher), a meter stick, wooden splints, and matches. (Enough material should be supplied so that students can work in teams of two.). Also include safety glasses for each student and for the teacher.

Investigation: The directions for carrying out this investigation instructed each team of students to fill the glass container of the Hoffman student-type apparatus one-third of the way with water and to fill the two test tubes with water, then to turn these tubes upside down into the water in the glass container so that the mouth of each test tube (full of water) was directly over one of the two electrodes. They then connected the electrodes to the direct current (DC) source. It was quickly apparent to students that nothing happened. That is, no change was observed.

The directions now called for adding $10\,cm^3$ of dilute sulfuric acid to the water, bathing the two electrodes. Students now observed that gas bubbles formed on the surfaces of the electrodes, inside the test tubes, with more bubbles collecting at one electrode than at the other. After a short period of observation, bubbles of gas began to escape from the electrodes and rise through the water into the test tubes, displacing the acidified water. Over time one test tube became totally filled with a colorless gas while the other tube filled only halfway with a colorless gas.

At this point, the directions called for disconnecting the DC source and checking the relative volumes of gas that had been collected using a ruler to compare the heights of the gas columns inside each tube. The results indicated a ratio of 2 to 1 in the volumes collected. Some students noted that the largest volume of gas had collected at the electrode labeled with a minus (–) sign. The tube over the electrode labeled plus (+) was the one that contained only half the volume of gas. Student observations at this point resulted in a number of inquiries. These were written down for future consideration.

The directions then called for removing the test tube that was completely filled with gas and holding it upside down while quickly thrusting a burning splint into the mouth of the tube. Students observed that the gas began to burn with a pale blue flame. The splint did not ignite again.

The directions then called for students to remove the second test tube from the water, allowing the water inside the tube to totally drain with the gas remaining. Following instructions, the students now turned this tube sideways and thrust a glowing splint into its mouth. Students immediately observed that the splint itself burst into flames, while the gas did not. The students quickly came to realize they were working with two completely different gaseous substances: one burned while the other supported burning. As a control, the students compared the results obtained by igniting another splint in air, noticing that it burned but not as profusely as the splint thrust into the second test tube.

Conclusions: The students were assigned to summarize, in writing, the procedure that had been followed as well as their observations of the results. In addition, the teacher requested that each team of students construct at least three inquiries or questions related to this investigation. In fact, students asked many questions orally that the teacher would not answer directly. Eventually, the many inquiries were shared across the teams, and a final list was prepared for posting on the query board. Examples of these follow:

- What are the two different gases called? How did they form? Does each have a chemical formula?

- Why are the properties of the two gases so different? Are burning and supporting burning chemical or physical properties?

- Why was twice as much of one gas, by volume, formed?

- Why didn't we use "regular" 120-volt AC house current?

- Why wasn't water affected by the electricity until we added acid to it?

- How did the small amount of acid, when added to the water, enable the solution to form the two gases, each with a different property?

- Why did the gas that collected at the minus (−) electrode actually burn while the gas that collected at the plus (+) electrode supported burning, similar to the burning of the splint in air?

- Are there names for these different electrodes? What makes them different?

- Is this electrical process also used to break-up substances other than water? What is the process called?

Extension: To enable students to respond to their inquiries and to develop explanations for the results observed in the investigation, the teacher supplied both hardcopy materials and Website names for the students to consult. While the students searched the references supplied, the teacher moved from group to group, occasionally responding to questions students raised about their readings. She also added several scientific terms to the "search and discover" list: *chemical catalysts, diatomic molecules, chemical equations, subscripts and coefficients,* and of course, *oxidation and reduction.* Eventually, results of students' explorations were shared across the entire class. Following is a brief summary of the discoveries that students made and submitted in their final reports:

1. The DC source of electricity resulted in the production of an anode (+) and a cathode (−); an excess of electrons at the (−) electrode, a lack of electrons at the (+) electrode. The electricity decomposed the water molecules to form hydrogen molecules at the cathode and oxygen molecules at the anode, but only when acid was added.

2. When exposed to a burning splint the hydrogen molecules reacted with oxygen molecules, present in the surrounding air, releasing enough heat energy to produce a flame. The oxygen molecules reacted with the cellulose and other molecules in the "energy rich" wooden splint to give off enough heat energy to cause the wood to burn, producing a flame.

Lesson 4b: Combining Hydrogen and Oxygen to Form Water

Student Learning Objectives:

- To build understanding that chemical changes or *reactions* can be made to occur in reverse

- To vividly demonstrate the absolute need for practicing safety procedures while learning in a chemistry laboratory setting

- To extend the practice of writing chemical symbols, chemical formulas, and chemical equations

- To gain practice in developing a scientific model using visual materials

Materials: Sources for both hydrogen and oxygen. (These can be obtained from cylinders of the gases if the school is licensed to purchase and house these sources.) The teacher prepared the two gases as follows:

- Oxygen: Prepared from hydrogen peroxide (39%) obtained at local drugstores and brewers' dry yeast obtained at local supermarkets

- Hydrogen: Prepared using mossy zinc and diluted hydrochloric acid

Each gas was produced in a gas generator and collected by water displacement using a pneumatic trough and a clean, pint-size milk paper carton. Other supplies were a three-foot-long taper, matches, a ruler, string, masking tape, a ring stand, and a ring or clamp. In addition were safety goggles for use by teacher and students, chemical lab aprons, and a clear plastic safety shield.

Method Demonstration: The teacher who performed this demonstration made certain that all students wore lab aprons and safety goggles covering their eyes. She did likewise, but in addition placed the clear plastic shield between the demonstration and the students.

She used the ruler to measure the distance two-thirds of the way down the side of the milk carton and marked this distance with masking tape. This was followed by tying string around the perimeter and close to the bottom of the carton, leaving enough string hanging to *eventually* tie the carton upside down to the ring that was attached to the ring stand.

She then filled the milk carton with water and placed it in the pneumatic trough partially filled with water so that the two gases could be collected in the carton by water displacement. This was followed by allowing the hydrogen to displace the water in the milk carton until the water level inside of the carton lowered to the mark made by the masking tape (two-thirds down the side of the carton). She followed this by displacing the remainder of the water (the final one-third of the volume of the milk carton) with oxygen. The carton now contained gasses in a ratio of two to one by volume.

The teacher then pinched the opening of the carton closed, turned the closed carton upside down, and tied it to the ring attached to the ring stand. Finally, she used a match to ignite the taper. Standing three feet away, she pointed the flame of the burning taper right next to the almost sealed mouth of the milk carton. An explosion resulted, splitting open the sides of the milk carton and causing an unforgettable, loud noise!

Following this, the teacher explained to the students that they had just observed how energy from the flame caused two elements to combine explosively, producing a release of energy. The result was the reverse of what the students had observed earlier in the electrolysis investigation. In that case, hydrogen and oxygen gasses were produced from water. In this case, water was produced, but in the form of invisible water vapor!

Follow-up to Demonstration: Student reaction to this demonstration was "Wow! We understand why you want us to take all kinds of safety measures when in the chemistry laboratory!" The students were assigned to summarize, in writing, what they learned from the demonstration and also to develop inquiries to be addressed in further class discussion. Examples of the inquiries included the following:

- "Why did you want to combine hydrogen and oxygen in a ratio of 2:1 by volume? Suppose you had used these two elements in the reverse ratio of 1:2 by volume; what would have happened?"

- "What happened to the water that was produced during this explosive reaction?"

- "How do we write the equation for this chemical reaction? It is the reverse of the reaction for the electrolysis of water, isn't it?"

- "Is there any place nearby that is using hydrogen fuel cells for energy?" (This teacher eventually took her classes to visit a local state college that did have a hydrogen fuel cell facility, partially funded by the state at $400,000. The college now produces 25 percent of its energy needs using such a fuel cell.)

Lesson 4c: Model Building

Investigation: To follow up on the lesson sequence described previously, the teacher had students construct visual models of the chemical reactions involved in both Lesson 4a and Lesson 4b. The students used Styrofoam balls of two sizes to represent H and O atoms and toothpicks to represent pairs of shared electrons between the atoms in H_2, O_2, and H_2O molecules (Figure 5.3). From being involved in this modeling activity, the students now began to understand the need for using subscripts and coefficients in writing equations for chemical reactions.

Conclusions: During the final segment of this introduction-to-chemistry unit, several teams of students volunteered to search for information on the following topics and report the results to the class:

- How reverse reactions can be represented by equations including the use of double arrows

- How energy is represented in chemical equations

- The meaning of the terms *oxidation* and *reduction*

- Robert Boyle's observation that led to a scientific law that indicates why gases all behave physically as they do, and how this understanding relates to using coefficients in equations for chemical reactions involving gases

- How chemical equations take into account the law of the conservation of matter

- The importance of O_2 in the air we breathe

- The importance of pure water to the world's human population

As readers might suspect, these student-prepared reports led to further student inquiries. The teacher devoted the final of the five class periods to this introduction to chemistry, including a summary of what the students had accomplished.

FIGURE 5.3

Model Demonstrating Hydrogen, Oxygen, and Water Molecules.

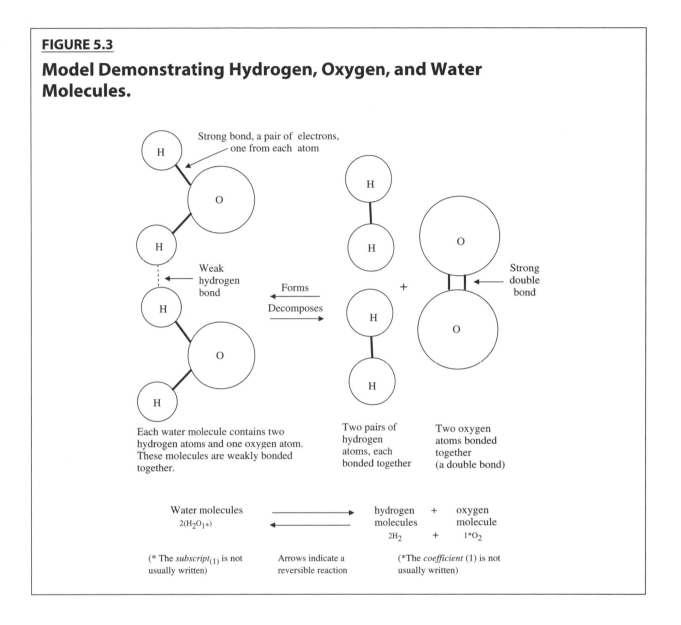

Each water molecule contains two hydrogen atoms and one oxygen atom. These molecules are weakly bonded together.

Two pairs of hydrogen atoms, each bonded together

Two oxygen atoms bonded together (a double bond)

Water molecules		hydrogen + oxygen
$2(H_2O_{1*})$		molecules molecule
		$2H_2$ + $1*O_2$

(* The *subscript*$_{(1)}$ is not usually written)

Arrows indicate a reversible reaction

(*The *coefficient* (1) is not usually written)

Comments on Lesson 4 (Study of Hydrogen, Oxygen, and Water)

The approach used in this lesson sequence was a very effective introduction to chemistry in that it enabled students to explore and develop a preliminary understanding of two essential chemical processes: oxidation and reduction. Although considerable instructional time was allocated to the initial investigation and the subsequent demonstration and follow-up activities, it was time well spent. This is the type of instruction that can serve to motivate and engage students in the study of chemistry, a subject often noted for being abstract and difficult. Although students carried out the electrolysis investigation, it was important to have the teacher demonstrate the procedure for the reverse reaction. Students will never forget this procedure. Should you decide to perform it yourself, you may want to inform your administrator about the loud noise that will be heard, especially during these times of concern for school security.

Lesson 5: Study of Oxidation and Reduction (Chemistry/Geology)

The following lesson was conducted as part of a larger unit titled "Introduction to Oxidation and Reduction." It started with a teacher demonstration, but as readers will quickly see, the teacher took advantage of student interest to extend the study beyond the usual realm. In this particular case, students learned how chemistry can be applied to a study of the earth sciences.

Student Learning Objectives:

- To apply the principle of oxidation and reduction to the reduction of a natural compound

- To understand the role of hydrogen as a reducing agent

- To develop understanding of how the study of chemistry and geology are related

- To extend students' inquiry/discovery skills

Method Demonstration: To ensure student safety, the instruction began with the teacher demonstrating the reduction of cupric oxide with hydrogen. The reaction was carried out in a 1.5-foot-long pyrex tube clamped horizontally to one or two ring stands. A one-hole stopper with a piece of tightly fitting glass tubing was placed into each end of the Pyrex tube after 10 grams of the oxide was placed in the center, inside the tube. Hydrogen gas from a cylinder of the compressed gas was then slowly fed through a rubber hose into the Pyrex tube until the tube was void of air and instead filled with hydrogen. The hydrogen was allowed to continue to flow from the tank slowly into the tube and to escape slowly into the air from the opposite end of the glass tube.

The teacher wore safety goggles and an apron, and placed a plastic shield in front of the setup as a "cautious protection". If such a demonstration is carefully planned and carried out, an explosion is extremely unlikely. Once the equipment was in place and the hydrogen given time to displace the air in the tube, the teacher directed a Bunsen burner flame to the underside of the Pyrex tube under the copper oxide. Within a few minutes, the students observed that the black cupric oxide began to turn to copper and a small amount of water vapor collected as a liquid on the inside of the far end of the Pyrex tube.

This very visual chemical change caused some students to inquire, "Can minerals like copper oxide be made from the metal? That is, for example, can the reverse occur?" The question was asked by a student who didn't realize that the rusting of iron to form iron oxide is an example of many ongoing processes during which metals become oxidized as the oxygen in the air becomes reduced.

Investigation: After the teacher's response, one student asked, "Can I try to make one of these minerals, malachite from copper?" She had become intrigued, especially with the natural-copper-containing-mineral malachite, because the instructor earlier had shown the class a sample of this blue-green mineral compound, which contains copper. He had polished the malachite into a pendant. He also had displayed other minerals that contain atoms of other metals. The teacher's response to the student's question was, of course, "Yes, but only if you are willing to keep the entire class informed of your progress." Together, the teacher and student developed a procedure for producing malachite. That procedure is included as Exhibit 5.2.

Conclusions: While the "volunteer" student was designing and carrying out the production of malachite, she and her peers were continuing to learn how to write and balance chemical equations that included the chemical equation for the reaction of copper oxide and hydrogen as well as equations for the reactions that led to the formation of the malachite.

As might be expected this one student's interest and enthusiasm led her classmates to raise many inquiries. The science teacher, and the student conducting the investigation, through careful planning, referred each inquiring student to an appropriate reference. Each discovery was eventually reported to the entire class. Here are a few examples of the students' inquiries:

- Why is malachite called a mineral?
- Does it have a chemical formula?
- Other than copper, of what elements does malachite consist?
- How do we know that the chemicals you are using to form malachite have the formulas that are indicated on the labels of the containers?
- What does USP on the bottle of $CaCO_3$ stand for?
- Where did all of these chemicals come from?
- What does the $3H_2O$ that is part of the formula for copper (2) nitrate indicate?
- How can we experimentally prove that the nitrate ions have H_2O bonded to them?

EXHIBIT 5.2

Procedure for Synthesizing the Mineral Malachite.

1. Begin the synthesis by preparing 250 ml of 0.5 molar $(Cu(NO_3)_2 \cdot 3H_2O$ (copper II nitrate trihydrate) solution. Note especially the color of this solution. Then place 25 ml of the solution into a 400 mL beaker.

2. Measure 40 mL of 1.0 molar NH_4OH (ammonium hydroxide) into a 100-mL graduated cylinder. Note the properties of this solution. Add the ammonium hydroxide to the 25 ml of the copper nitrate solution and stir the mixture, noting the results. Now add the remainder of the 1.0 molar NH_4OH solution and continue to stir the mixture. Again, observe any changes. (On the basis of the observations that you have made thus far, write at least two inquiries to which you will be seeking answers.)

3. Use a 250-mL graduated cylinder to measure 150 mL of carbonated or seltzer water or club soda. (Either of these drinks is basically a saturated solution of CO_2 and H_2O. The solution serves mainly to supply carbonate ions (CO_3^{2-}).

4. Add the 150 mL of CO_3^{2-} solution to the original mixture and stir it. Pour the resulting solution equally into four large test tubes. Place the test tubes with the solution into a large beaker of boiling water for a period of twenty minutes.

5. Allow the four tubes with their contents to cool. Then, using a filtering funnel, filter the material from each test tube onto a sheet of filter paper. Place each piece of filter paper, with its contents, open on a watch glass to dry overnight.

6. While the samples are drying, use the *Handbook of Mineralology* or another appropriate reference to find the physical and chemical properties of the malachite you have prepared.

7. Use one of the dried samples to determine each of the properties indicated below and compare your results to those formed in the available mineral handbook.

   A. *Specific gravity:* Weigh one of the four dry samples. Then place this sample into a graduated cylinder and add exactly 10.0 ml of water. Determine in this way the volume of the sample. The specific gravity is the mass of the substance divided by the volume it occupies (compared to the density of water).

   B. *pH:* Carefully wash a second sample of the dried substance with a small portion of water. Then place the washed sample into a clean mortar and add 25 ml of distilled water. With a clean pestle, gently crush and grind the sample into the water. This grinding will allow some of the dry substance to dissolve in the water. After about five minutes of grinding, test the water with pH-hydrion paper to obtain the pH of the solution. Write an inquiry about the results you obtain and then answer this question.

   C. *Reaction with acid:* From your past experience in chemistry, predict what will occur when you add 15 to 20 mL of 0.1 molar hydrochloric acid (HCl) to one of the remaining dry samples that you first placed in a test tube. Add the acid and determine if your prediction is correct. Then explain the results.

   D. *Effect of heat:* Observe a sample of natural malachite. If this is not available, study a colored photograph of a multitinted layered specimen. Develop an inquiry about the layers you see and discuss with the class members possible answers to your and their inquiries. Now gently heat the last of the four original samples by first placing it into a clean evaporating dish. Heat the sample and observe what happens to the colors of the sample. Explain a cause for some of the layers in natural malachite to vary in color intensity. Indicate two or three substances that might produce these layers. Give reasons for selecting each of the substances.

   Compare the results of each of the four tests above to information obtained from the mineral handbook.

- Why does a compound appear dry if it has water bonded to its particles?

- What is the electronic structure for the Cu^{2+} ion, and what makes it blue?

- Do we run across any of these chemicals (such as H_2CO_3) in our daily lives? Can metallic copper be extracted from malachite? If so, how is it done?

- Can we learn more about the history of malachite? Where is it mined? Is it a true compound that follows the law of definite composition? I read in the Bible about the "Stone of Eliat"—was this stone Malachite?

EXHIBIT 5.3

History Related to the Mineral Malachite: A Summary.

One of the most beautiful of minerals that has been used as jewelry by people since early civilizations is the blue-green mineral malachite. This mineral is found in dry or semi-arid regions in the Earth's crust. Chemists have discovered from laboratory investigations that malachite is a basic carbonate of copper whose chemical formula is $CuCO_3 \cdot Cu(OH)_2$.

King Solomon's copper mines, 3,000 to 4,000 years ago, are referred to in the Old Testament of the Bible. These mines still exist in the Sinai Desert in the Middle East near the City of Eliat. Tourists to this region today can purchase "Stones of Eliat," which are stones that contain malachite.

Besides jewelry, malachite has been ground into fine powder to form a green pigment used in making paints used by early artists.

Malachite, in its natural state, has a hardness of 3.5 to 4.0 on the Mohs Scale. This mineral consists of a number of layers of varying tints of green or blue with some black streaks. These different colors are due to chemical compounds other than the copper carbonate that is present and to the changing conditions that existed over the thousands or millions of years as the minerals formed. These conditions, including varying amounts of oxygen, carbon dioxide, and moisture, along with temperature changes, have resulted in these compounds, all of which contain copper.

In the early 1800's, chemists had heated disagreements over the characteristics of the many chemical compounds and mixtures that were found in the Earth's crust. A scientist of the era, Claude Louis Bertholette, published his understanding of the composition of chemical compounds. He concluded that the composition of elements in certain compounds can vary within certain limits. Joseph Louis Proust, who determined the chemical composition of a number of minerals, among them malachite, concluded, however, that the weight of the various elements making up this mineral is always the same regardless of where the mineral comes from. According to Proust, Bertholette's earlier conclusion needed to be modified. This conclusion led Proust in 1808 to state his famous *Law of Definite Proportions* or *Definite Composition*, ending, for the time being, a long-standing controversy or confusion over the difference between mixtures and chemical compounds.

Even prior to the controversy, Jeremiah Benjamin Richter created the term *stoichiometry*, to mean the "measurement of the proportions by weight of the chemical elements in chemical compounds."

Today, we know that The Law of Definite Composition holds true, except for compounds that contain isotopes of the same elements. Different forms of chemical bonding of elements in compounds also lead to exceptions to this law.

Some of the inquiries posed by the class were addressed in a report summarizing the history of malachite written by the lead student. Her report drew on several references, including *Dan's Manual of Mineralogy* (1949). She also consulted Websites that included information about minerals, ores, industrial processes for extracting copper, copper mining, and so on, as well as historical information about the law of definite proportions. The report was eventually distributed to each class member (Exhibit 5.3).

Comments on Lesson 5 (Study of Oxidation and Reduction)

In this lesson we saw how one student can catalyze further inquiry/discovery classroom-wide. With one student proposing a new topic for study, her decision was supported by the remainder of the class and, of course, by the teacher. Clearly, her investigation, the classroom discussion surrounding it, and the reporting of it engaged both the student and her classmates in the scientific enterprise, which encompasses experimentation, discovery, sharing of information, and thinking about applications of scientific principles. The exploration of the historical background by the single student, shared with classmates, gave an additional dimension to the experience. We leave it up to the readers to assign an appropriate level of inquiry/discovery to this experience!

We can report an exciting follow-up to this case history. The student and teacher eventually published the procedure for the malachite synthesis that they had developed (Exhibit 5.2) in the journal *Chemistry* (Schmuckler and Snyder, 1975). Today, this former student is a science teacher and chairperson of the science department at a large urban high school, designing and teaching programs that are motivating more students to inquire and discover and eventually for some to enter scientific fields.

Summary

This chapter included case histories of science instruction at higher levels of inquiry/discovery that are appropriate for high school–level students. Each of the lesson sequences addressed the inquiry/discovery process or "inquiry" standards referred to at the beginning of the chapter as well as other content-learning objectives. Each lesson sequence offered a somewhat different approach to addressing the standards, and they incorporated varied examples of content. The final lesson sequence included an opportunity for students to briefly share in exploring the history of science, emphasizing that scientists search for simple explanations and develop laws that describe natural occurrences. These theories and laws, as indicated, are subject to continual change as knowledge about the environment in which humans live increases. This historical component enriches the outcomes of student involvement in each investigation. And this history supports students in learning to understand the nature of the scientific enterprise, including the significant role that the inquiry/discovery processes play in this enterprise.

Chapter 6

Supportive Instruction in Language and Team Building

IN SPRING OF EVERY YEAR SINCE 1951, as Madeleine Jacobs informs us in "On the Nature of Discovery" (2003), Nobel Laureates have been meeting in Lindau, Germany, to address the characteristics of the discovery process that led to the findings that warranted their receiving Nobel Prizes. Jacobs notes that "promising young people are invited to these meetings so that they might learn from the high-level interaction. During the sessions, the Laureates often refer to the development of a healthy, skeptical and creative habit of mind, ascribing to the belief that this habit of mind is the outgrowth of science literacy, an important factor in the development of knowledgeable, effective learners. Phrases like: *doubt, difficult, unpredictable*, and *full of surprises* pervade the discussions. Using such descriptors, the Laureates address what they personally have come to understand about the process of making their discoveries. They conclude the ability to discover is not usually self-taught. It develops or is strengthened through practice, especially during schooling." The implications of this conclusion are sobering. If school-level experiences are inappropriate, the ability and willingness of students to eventually inquire and discover on their own, or to discover within a group setting, may not materialize.

The Scope of Inquiry/Discovery

The cyclic nature of *student inquiry* and *discovery* during instruction leads to this definition for the *student discovery* process: Student discovery (in instruction) is the result of students learning to *investigate*, searching for answers *to their own inquiries*. These skills include the traditional set: observing, reasoning, measuring, mathematically manipulating data, preparing tables of data and graphs and interpreting these, and drawing conclusions from those findings. Important additional discovery skills that are not historically associated with science instruction include the following "language" skills: *wondering, explaining, discussing, reading, writing, editing,* and *revising*. This last group of discovery skills is emphasized because they must be considered with the other more traditional discovery skills; without them, the learning of science through investigations cannot effectively occur.

In 1995 David Haury, then director of the ERIC Center for Science, Mathematics and Environmental Education at Ohio State University, developed the "Circle of Inquiry" shown in Figure 6.1. This circle includes the word *inquiry* at its center, surrounded by sixty-three skills practiced in association with or during science investigations. What Haury refers to as "discovery process skills" are *student inquiries* (questions related to investigating)

FIGURE 6.1

The Circle of Inquiry.

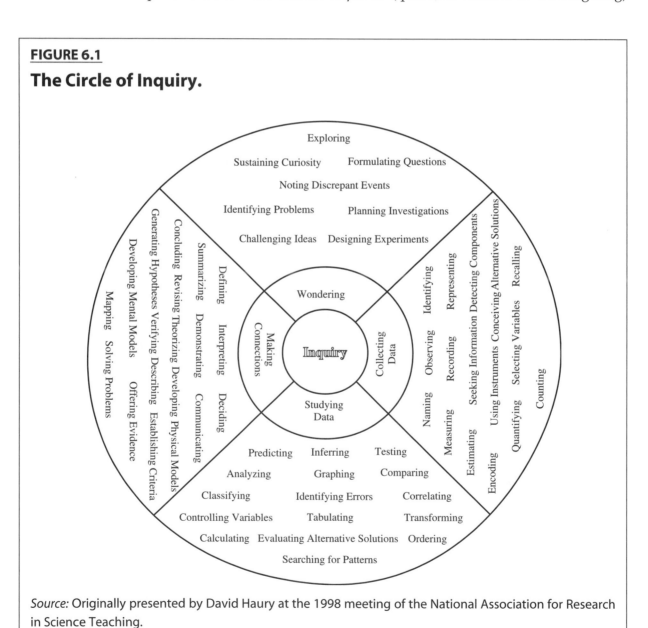

Source: Originally presented by David Haury at the 1998 meeting of the National Association for Research in Science Teaching.

that create opportunities for *students* to practice the four *student-discovery skills* indicated in the first circle outside of the center of the "Circle of Inquiry": *wondering, collecting data, studying data*, and *making connections*. The emphasis on *students* is what makes this set of skills essential.

Notice that unlike Bloom's Taxonomy, discussed further on, Haury's Circle does not attempt to organize or compartmentalize the skills listed, merely allocating them to specific areas of inquiry. J. H. Arter and J. R. Salman of the Northwest Regional Education Laboratory indicate additional skills in their publication *Assessing Higher Order Thinking Skills: A Consumers' Guide* (1987). Furthermore, they organize discovery skills by dividing them into higher-order skills—"formulating alternative solutions" and "comparing similarities and differences"—then dividing them into six subgroups: (1) problem solving, (2) decision making, (3) inferring, (4) divergent thinking, (5) evaluative skills, (6) philosophical reasoning.

Students cannot effectively practice the *discovery skills* above without the ability to use higher levels of language. The reverse is also true: designing instruction so that students have opportunities to discover answers to their own inquiries through investigation provides an excellent way to increase students' language literacy.

Importance of Language in Inquiry / Discovery Education

Too often we as teachers compartmentalize what we offer students because it is simpler to plan lessons when we only need to consider our own specialty. We assume students will be able to "see" that they cannot study science without math skills or without using language to support their learning; however, most students do not see those connections. Thus compartmentalizing instruction has produced students with compartmentalized minds: for example, students do not believe that they need to use their language arts skills in writing paragraphs describing science discoveries. If inquiry/discovery instruction is to succeed, it is essential for teachers to eliminate the artificial partitions that education has created among disciplines. A way to dismantle those barriers is for teachers across disciplines to link their classrooms in mutually beneficial activities. For example, because science presents a very complex vocabulary, it is important to assist students with "word attack" skills; teaching them that historically the core languages (Latin and Greek) have been used to create new words as science "unfolds," reiterating the need to expand its vocabulary, bringing additional relevance to the task. The language arts teacher is an important resource here: a science teacher who needs assistance with teaching vocabulary development can consult that colleague to find a data bank of root words and their meanings, and make suggestions for ways to develop appropriate science vocabulary activities in preparation for the SATs, for example, and for vocabulary building as a lifelong skill.

Developing Student-Generated Higher Orders of Inquiry or Questioning

In an earlier chapter we referred to the fact that, paradoxically, young children often ask higher-order questions. Experience indicates that they stop asking such questions by the time they reach the fourth grade. (We surmise this happens because parents and teachers discourage such questions either because they are unable to answer them or they consider them to be irrelevant. Because they ignore or discourage formulation of questions on those levels, children give up asking them.) The net result is that children and adults alike are usually unable to respond successfully when asked to formulate higher-order questions beginning with words such as *why* and *how*. In the inquiry/discovery classroom, helping students redevelop their *questioning* skills is essential to the development of successful inquiries. Benjamin Bloom's Taxonomy (Exhibit 6.1) provides a word bank of verbs to use in structuring inquiry, but questions need more than verbs. Nouns and phrases, such as those listed in the "Basic Inference Skills Diagram" and the "Inference Skills Diagram" (Figures 6.2 and 6.3, which appear later in this chapter), become the basis for the types of questions that identify relationships among information gathered, and are the basis for conclusions drawn during investigations.

Exhibit 6.1, "Blooming Verbs," offers examples of action words associated with each of the three basic cognitive levels of understanding, from the lowest level, "recalls," to the highest level, "problem solves." This exhibit provides action verbs that, when employed during inquiries, cause those involved in the inquiry process to *expect* different levels of responses. The first level simply expects responses that involve remembering facts (the who, what, when, where). The next higher level, "compares/contrasts," acknowledges the expectation that the response links new information to what is already known (how). The third level demands responses that test new information against existing understanding(s) (why). That is, inquiries at this highest level lead to conclusions based on evidence or critical support, or lead to justification of a position that has been taken, or to realization that the initial conclusion is unsupported by evidence. It is at this highest level that both students and teachers require the most practice. This level of inquiry exemplifies scientific thinking that reflects the nature of the scientific enterprise itself!

The importance of this statement is indicated in the July 7, 2005, issue of *Science*, honoring the journal's 125th year of publication with the special

---

EXHIBIT 6.1

"Blooming Verbs from Bloom's Taxonomy" or "Bloom's Taxonomy Verbalized."

Each inquiry requires the use of one or more action verbs that clearly state the task for the information the questioner seeks to acquire. That task should demonstrate not only "knowledge" to be sought and discovery to be gained, but also the extension of that knowledge. Examples of verbs and their relationship to each increasing level of inquiry are indicated below.

Cognitive Level 1, Recalls (C-1)

Knowledge *states* because it *defines, describes, identifies, labels, lists, matches, names, outlines, selects, tells, writes.*

It has a specific, limited purpose of recalling to mind what is already known.

Comprehension *explains* because it *distinguishes, estimates, exemplifies, extends, generalizes, paraphrases, points out, summarizes.*

It has the specific function of clarifying new information so that it can be assimilated into the existing body of knowledge.

Cognitive Level 2, Compares/Contrasts (C-2)

Application *demonstrates* because it *changes, computes, converts, discovers, illustrates, links, manipulates, modifies, operates, prepares, produces, relates, reproduces, shows, solves, uses.*

It has the specific function of linking new information to the existing body of knowledge.

Analysis *categorizes* because it *breaks down, combines, compares, contrasts, defends, diagrams, differentiates, distinguishes, examines, infers, organizes, separates, subdivides.*

It has the specific function of organizing new information into the existing body of knowledge.

Cognitive Level 3, Problem Solves (C-3)

Synthesis *groups* because it *compiles, composes, creates, designs, devises, generates, interprets, modifies, plans, predicts, rearranges, reconstructs, relates, relegates, reorganizes, revises.*

It has the specific function of testing new information against the existing body of knowledge.

Evaluation *appraises* because it *concludes, criticizes, discriminates, eliminates, generalizes, justifies, supports.*

It has the specific function of integrating new information with the existing body of knowledge already possessed.

---

section "What Don't We Know," especially the article by T. Siegfried, "In Praise of Hard Questions." The article considers 125 of these questions, including, for example, "To what extent are genetic variations and personal health linked?" "How much can human life be extended?" "How did cooperative behavior evolve?" "Will Malthus continue to be wrong?" Neither scientists' efforts to design and undertake such inquiries, nor efforts of the teachers and their students who emulate them, mean that asking questions at the factual information level is unimportant. It does mean, however, that teachers must constantly recommit themselves to searching for opportunities for students to go beyond the factual information level, to practice asking and answering the higher-order questions that link facts in new ways, especially in relation to their science investigations.

Science teachers have the advantage of offering students opportunities to search for and discover answers to higher-order questions through actual experiences and direct observations. Language teachers, working closely with science teachers, can offer students opportunities to ask higher-order questions by introducing students to printed reference materials, legitimate Websites, and appropriate historic literature that may provide conflicting positions on scientific issues for evaluation. Teachers of inquiry/discovery need to procure such references through their own readings and interaction with knowledgeable specialists. Samples of sources for such resources are offered in Appendix A.

The authors encourage teachers of both subjects to place enlarged copies of Exhibit 6.1 on their classroom walls to be referred to repeatedly during discussions and activities. You also may reproduce copies of this exhibit for students to carry in their notebooks for reference as they improve their communication skills and thought processes.

Implementing Higher-Order Student Questioning

Following are case histories that describe how teachers overcame students' problems with designing appropriate higher-order questions, thus greatly improving learning outcomes.

Case History I: Completing Assignments

As a beginning teacher, I asked many questions, often receiving blank stares rather than answers. For example, I would ask my students, "Do you have any questions about the homework assigned?" Often there was no response, so I simply moved on. Then, when the assignment was due, the same students had many reasons for not completing it, including all the questions they had not asked when given the opportunity. Finally I came upon a resolution to this dilemma. I told my classes that students would not ever be excused from completing an assignment because they did not understand it. However, if the assignment was difficult, they could come to class with three very specific written questions about the nature of the assignment. An example of such a student question might be, "Were we to answer all four questions or just select one from the four?" Students who had completed the work assigned handed in their papers. Those students received credit for completing the work as well as extra credit for orally explaining how they knew what to do.

Students with questions were required to write down the answers given to their questions. The "non-understanders" were expected to complete the assignment by the next class period. If they completed the assignment then, they received full credit for handing in the homework with their answered three questions. I used the same strategy for addressing "no response" to in-class questions. The activity held students accountable both for their assignments and for creating questions to achieve understanding of what was expected of them. It also rewarded students who accepted responsibility for understanding their assignments before starting them. I learned to restructure my instruction to require students to inquire more, orally and in writing, before starting an assignment, thus reducing the number of blank stares and late or no responses to both classwork and out-of-class assignments.

At Back to School Nights and during parent conferences I shared my approach with parents, who reported they found it helpful when assisting their children with confusing assignments, especially when the parents were at a loss as well. They instructed their children to write down specific questions about the assignment to ask their teachers the next day. Then the parents added brief notes confirming the effort expended by the students and signed them. We all were much less frustrated using this approach.

I also learned to send students to appropriate topical references where they could find answers to their questions. I learned that, at times, I had to support my students by helping them restructure their questions. This practice led to my asking myself, then finding answers for, the following questions:

- *What parts of the assignments(s) can my students handle without my support?* (In other words, What parts are most clearly related to what we have addressed during previous assignment(s) and activities?)

- *What part(s) of the assignment(s) confused the students?* (In other words, What new delimiters have been added to the instructions that make this assignment different and scary or confusing to students? How could I redesign the questions to ensure that the students could handle them?)

- *What information did students need to know already in order for them to successfully find answers?* (In other words, How could students be assured that what they now know would see them successfully through new material?)

- *Where did it make sense to look for answers?* (In other words, What information or procedures had we gathered that would provide assistance to students as they pursued these answers?)

This early experience has resulted in my teaching becoming more effective in terms of student learning and in students' interest in the subject.

Case History II: Improving Students' Grades

Through the experience described in this case history, a student became motivated to improve his level of inquiring and learning, and the teacher applied the strategy developed to assisting other students in her classes.

Pat was a "B" student who, one day after class, approached me, asking, "Why don't I ever get an 'A' from you (or from my other teachers)?"

He, in fact, was a model student who participated in class discussions and asked questions. He submitted his assignments on time and generally was conscientious. So what was missing? I thought for a moment, especially about the nature of his questions and answers during that class period, and concluded, "Pat, you do ask questions and give answers. However, they all are at low levels of cognitive thinking."

Unsurprisingly, Pat's response was, "Huh?" So I explained, "Pat, you limit your questions and answers to those that begin with the words *who*, *what*, *when*, and *where*. Questions of this type are factual, dead ends. You need to practice expanding your thinking to questions that begin with words like *why* and *how*. Those questions and their answers lead to further discussion and higher-order thinking as well as deeper understandings. Instead of leading to closure, they open us up for additional questioning and learning."

I drew a rough sketch of what *limited* and *more expanded* "looked like" (Figure 6.2). "Notice," I said, "that the use of the words *who, what, when*, and *where* causes you to think in circles. If you ask questions about *how* and *why*, the ideas spiral upward, providing opportunities for limitless learning! As an example, we have been studying about the impact of uncovering the genome. You asked who discovered this and when did it happen? You need also to ask, 'Why is this discovery so important, and what would have happened if the discovery had not occurred?' Then you need to search for answers to such questions. Knowing when and who alone will fade from your memory, but knowing why and how will lead to further inquiries and knowledge, to longer-term understandings, and to that 'A' you want."

Pat pointed out that that was difficult to do and even a little scary. I agreed with him, but explained that risk-taking was part of the growth process for learners. If there were no risks, there would be little gained from the experience. Such risk-taking was characteristic of the "A" student he wished to be.

FIGURE 6.2

Basic Inference Skills Diagram.

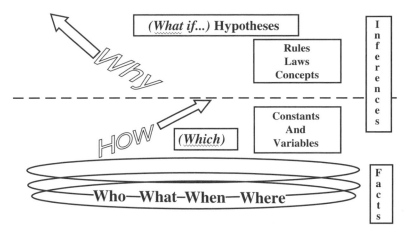

Notes: The lower part of this figure portrays the development of student inquiry at the most basic level, with the need for an "escape" route that can be used to free them from circular thinking in order to attain the higher levels of Inquiry. Adding the key word *which* demands that they begin to make judgments based on observation and analysis. As indicated, that leads to recognition of factors that are constant to each situation (mathematical formulas, for example) and to the variables that will lead to further investigation. Merely asking "why" does not, as every child has learned, produce answers that lead to discovery of the rules that govern the way variables change.

The experience was rewarding for both of us. Pat did begin to search beyond lower levels of questioning, which kept me "on my toes" in order to be of continuing support.

• • •

Pat used what he learned about questioning to become an "A" student. His teacher also learned from that experience that students needed to learn how to "see" questions and what they were being asked to focus on in their answers. Through experimentation, that basic diagram evolved into a series of sentence stems for questions to help trigger the kinds of thinking students were expected to generate.

From then on, early in each school year, Pat's teacher introduced her students to the visual diagram shown in Figure 6.3, "Inference Skills Diagram." Then each student was provided with his or her own copy of the diagram to refer to and was shown how to use the key words and phrases as "stems" for appropriate questions during discussions. A period was spent developing questions based on the diagram and answering them as they related to a current lesson, accompanied by an explanation of their "worth"

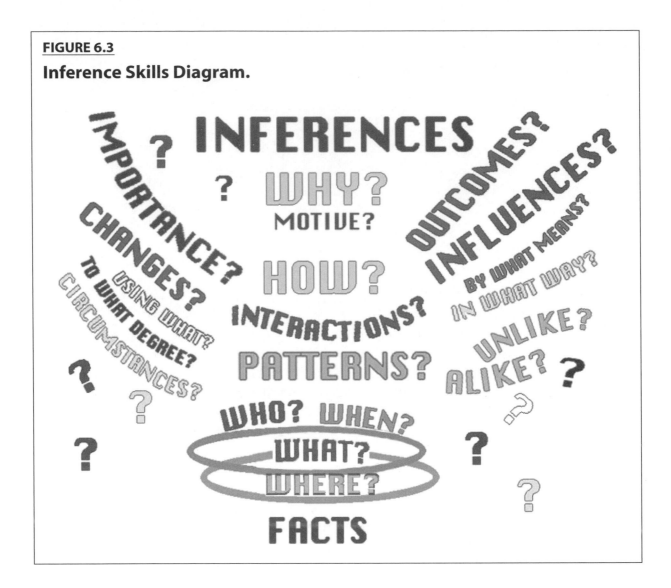

FIGURE 6.3

Inference Skills Diagram.

in terms of Bloom's Taxonomy. For the remainder of the year, the class continued to model use of the diagram during open-ended discussions and in devising review questions for summative assessments. This simple visual representation proved an effective way to lead to increased numbers of students getting into the habit of asking and answering higher-order questions. The teacher's task became one of supporting those students as they searched for appropriate references and investigations to use to find answers to these higher-order questions and to formulate additional inquiries.

Question Cubes

A colleague had a unique technique for helping students find ways to use the stems portrayed in Figure 6.3. She had students construct "question cubes" with various question stems on them (see Figure 6.4 for one

FIGURE 6.4

Model of the Question Cube.

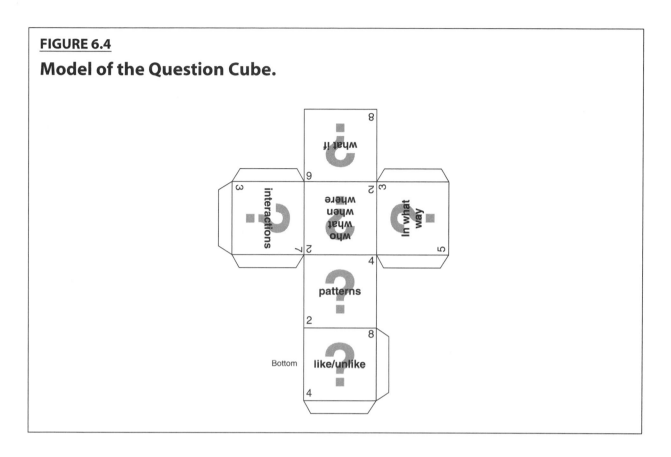

example). Once the cubes were constructed, during the current investigation, the students rolled them and made questions with the revealed stems. They could use the stems revealed to them (from where they were sitting) on any of the cubes at their tables. The paired numbers placed on the cubes represented the number of points they could accumulate for providing answers to the questions generated, depending on the appropriateness of the questions to the activity.

Another colleague modified the idea further by having his students create cubes with just the levels of Bloom's Taxonomy on each side: *Know* (facts), *Understand* (identify), *Apply* (example), *Analyze* (relationship), *Synthesize* (compare/contrast), and *Evaluate* (problem solve). His students were encouraged to use both the Taxonomy verbs (Exhibit 6.1) and the Inference Skills Diagram (Figure 6.3) to create their questions. The students followed the procedures described above to use the cubes.

Helping Students Understand the Sources of Assessment Questions

Too often when students express amazement upon seeing specific questions on summative assessments, teachers are amazed as well. The teachers' amazement stems from the awareness that, although the students have not recognized their presence, both those questions and their answers have been presented in many forms throughout the unit activities. Thus it is important to help students generate questions themselves, not only so they can expand their own knowledge through the seeking of answers, but also so that they are prepared when others demand those answers from them. A tool that helps them develop this skill is the "question quilt," presented here as Exhibit 6.2. This format is extremely useful because it helps students focus on the degree of sophistication expected from them in their answers and helps them understand why questions are awarded different point values, depending on their complexity and the level of thinking skills involved in answering them.

No matter what technique is used to help students develop effective questioning skills and promote the desire to find answers, the more unique the approach the greater interest students have in participation, as can be seen from the example that follows.

Case History III: Pointing the Way to Higher-Order Questioning Skills

I developed a discussion "game" in which students received points from 1 to 50 based on the order of their inquiries: Simple factual recall questions received 1 point; questions involving examples received 5 to 10 points, depending on their complexity; 20 points were awarded for questions that demanded linking up ideas and concepts; and 50 points were awarded for questions that demanded statements of "laws" or conclusions describing major relationships or concepts, or refined aspects of those laws ("What if …?" for example). Students were encouraged to use the "Inference Skills Diagram" (Figure 6.3) to help them formulate their questions. During the discussion, students were awarded an equal number of points for *answering* those questions. Partial answers received points appropriate for the level of response given, and students were able to "piggyback" on those answers to increase the "value" of the cumulative response attained.

The announcement of the number of points awarded for key questions prodded other students to inquire about the inquiry process. The discussion that ensued was twofold: "Why was that a 20-point (or 50-point) question?" represented one side, and answers to the questions presented was the second. That provided opportunities to develop metacognition, discussions of why some questions were more helpful than others, not only in science but also in general. Students soon developed the knack of asking higher-order questions and found they enjoyed the hunt for "50-point" answers to them. They also found it intriguing that, as in real life, the sum of the values for questions that it took to "build" to a 50-point question might be far greater than 50 points. That observation led to a discussion of

EXHIBIT 6.2

The Question Quilt.

Questions created and posted by students for a particular unit of study and displayed in the classroom for review can be outlined in this format

Bloom's Level	Questions Week 1	Questions Week 2	Questions Week 3	Questions Week 4	Questions Week 5
Recall (Often broken down into Knowledge and Comprehension)	Label the parts of the human cell.	Define in writing the word *mitochondria.*	Name three functions of the nucleus of an animal cell.	Who coined the term *cell*?	Match the structure with the function of the listed parts.
Application	Categorize the cell structures as plant, animal, or both.	?	?	?	?
Analysis	Compare and contrast plant and animal cells.	?	?	?	?
Synthesis	Using the graph, predict the influence of salt water on the celery (plant) cells.	?	?	?	?
Evaluation	Argue that cell size is limited and that number of cells determines size of animals.	?	?	?	?

Source: Butler and McMunn, 2006, citing McMunn and Schenck, 1996.

the kinds of "connections" that James Burke propounded so beautifully in his 1979 PBS series of the same name. It became a chance to emphasize that much of our scientific knowledge has come from the ability to see relationships, to find such connections or linkages, even among materials apparently unrelated to the current issue.

To be assured that your students understand the concept of higher orders of inquiry, take time with them to associate a sampling of action skills or verbs included in the "Inference Skills Diagram" (Figure 6.3). Point out how the various relationships are aligned with the level of question with which they are most strongly associated, and compare the diagram with those levels indicated in Exhibit 6.1. Taking this time to compare and contrast the two listings will lead to a greater probability that your students will discover the "power" of searching for and using more effective verbs and relationship descriptors as you design higher orders of inquiries.

Working with Students in Teams

The transition to the inquiry/discovery classroom requires rethinking of the parameters of a teacher's role. It is not unusual for a teacher making the transition to ask, "OK, the *kids* are asking questions, initiating the activities, researching related topics, finding connections; what am *I* doing?" It is a good question. The shift demands that the teacher restructure his or her own activities and view of his or her role in the classroom. True, the teacher is described as the "guide on the side" or the "mentor" of students as they work, but his or her greater role is as *assessor* of the skills and procedures students initiate and use. Teachers also devise the appropriate framework within which student activities are structured and evaluated. So, they must generate a whole new sequence of personal activities to undertake as students work. In Chapter Seven, suggestions are made for ways in which teachers can direct their attention to those modifications. Here it is important to note that teachers make available to students a variety of procedures that focus their attention and provide them with techniques for achieving success. Several possibilities are described in the following section. It is necessary to note there are many more options available, and that these can be accessed by any teacher who diligently uses Websites to find appropriate teaching and assessment tools.

Please note that the majority of these activities are collaborative—team centered—because students learn best when they support each other in the attainment of new information and skills. These activities also provide opportunities for more successful students to model their practices, and for other students to actually ask for assistance in developing those skills as they work, rather than waiting for one mentor (the teacher) to arrive to delegate the activities. An incentive for peer assistance, rather than merely taking over the task, is to provide extra credit for those who lend a "helping hand" to others as they work. Furthermore, it is essential to note that these practices only work effectively with groups that are heterogeneously grouped. If all of the successful (or unsuccessful) students are grouped together, no one can really gain from supporting each other's activity. In addition, in the workplace adults are expected to be team players, supporting each other as they achieve common goals. Students need to "buy into" those assumptions so that they already know how to respond effectively to those demands before they join that workforce.

The Peer Teaching Approach to Instruction

This approach involves pairing students so that they can effectively work together when they are learning new material, teaching and assisting each other. It is essentially an extension of the "Think/Pair/Share" approach recommended by Frank Lyman of the University of Maryland (www.readingquest.org/strat/tps.html), among others. In each group, when the students have varying academic capabilities, the more academically advanced students, who master new material more readily, monitor and teach those students in the group who have more difficulty in learning. As the less advanced students become more knowledgeable, they regroup themselves by finding other students with whom they can pool their strengths. Using this approach, the instructor serves as a facilitator, as is true in overall inquiry/discovery-oriented instruction. When students become stumped by their peers' inquiries, the teacher obtains the necessary sources of information or guidelines for students to use in response to their group's inquiries. Thus the teacher involves individual students as well as groups in the inquiry process and in reporting the discoveries made.

The Jigsaw Approach

Using this approach, students work in groups as they practice inquiry/discovery skills in a way that results in "peer teaching." As the term *jigsaw* implies, the group members' tasks are appropriately organized so that each student's role is unique, as is each group's, so that the group and class cannot function effectively without each other. For this approach to work efficiently, each student is required to read or examine a segment of the required work, asking and answering questions for that assigned portion, followed by group members sharing the gathered information with the rest of the group, then with the class. It is important that each segment of instruction be understandable independent of other segments. Therefore, sequential information that is dependent on having read or learned a previous segment is not suitable for use.

Brainstorming versus Hypothesizing

In this approach, students are motivated to learn science and to develop related language skills by making predictions despite having little prior knowledge of the proposed subject. The strategy encourages students to experiment with hunches and "no fault" intuitive thought processing. (It is important to make clear, especially to more able students, that this approach is *not* the same as hypothesizing, which is based on logically reasoned ideas about *probable* outcomes. Substantial knowledge and understanding of a subject are essential to hypothesizing, whereas brainstorming involves students considering inquiries about variables or factors that *might* need to be considered in designing a future investigation. Unlike in hypotheses, realistic parameters are not a concern.) It is important that all judgmental responses are withheld during the process, and all contributions are treated as though they were viable, however "off the wall" they might appear. Only later, when investigating possibilities, are parameters created that "rule out" the most bizarre of the options suggested. For example, it was brainstorming that resulted in the creation of Velcro, an outcome of identifying the way briars use "hooks" to affix themselves to transient forms, thus transporting seeds to new locations.

Hitchhiking

This instructional approach encourages students to "tag along" with others who are brainstorming or hypothesizing in response to an inquiry. They assist others as they offer higher-order questions and approaches to use in creating procedures to be followed during investigation. For example, after the inquiry is initiated, other students ask questions related to factors that should be taken into account in designing a follow-up investigation.

When the initial student's question is raised, a student "note taker" is assigned to write the question on a transparency or on the board. As additional student "hitchhikers" become aware of ways to expand the original inquiry, they may snap their fingers to signal that they wish to "hitch a ride." That is, they are offering to provide valuable input to the discussion, either to suggest additional inquiries or identify areas of investigation that may clarify the issue being discussed. The inquiries or suggestions posed by the hitchhiking students are added to the list, so that the entire class can visualize all of the related suggestions. Because this process initially also involves brainstorming, all of the students' inquiries and suggestions are written without being edited for appropriate grammar or syntax by the teacher or by fellow students. Unrelated ideas and grammatical and spelling errors remain, because, at this point, it is the uninterrupted flow of ideas that is important. As questions are generated, classmates listen, respond, and search for clues or answers, either by reading articles located by the teacher or students that relate to the topic being considered or by going online to find information. Once again, they "snap," then announce their plan of action. Eventually, the teacher halts the "ride," and, with the students, addresses the need to modify or eliminate questions that are not clearly related to designing inquiry. In the process the class corrects grammar and spelling and organizes the materials. Those who have already begun investigations report their findings. The greatest value of this approach is developing students' risk-taking abilities, their ability to "think outside the box" or take a chance on intuition as a guide to further exploration.

Brainstorming and hitchhiking together can result in promoting student understanding that effective listening and reading are cooperative skills that result in improved student learning. The "suspension" of limits, purposefully facilitated by the teacher who has encouraged risk-taking, frees students from structures that might otherwise limit their learning. Through the use of the strategies together, students become aware that creative thinking is essential if ideas are to lead to future inquiries. The thought processes associated with brainstorming and hitchhiking can result in entirely new avenues of investigation and produce useful learning.

Mind Mapping

This approach to instruction very personally involves students with materials being analyzed during instruction. It begins with the teacher supplying each student (or small group of students) with a large sheet of blank paper on which the students "map out" an illustration of their responses to their reading as they develop order among ideas or events that, at first, may seem disparate or unrelated. The creator of each map selects the visual tools that are most suited to his or her thinking about a subject and the relationships of its various components. Mind mapping follows no prescribed "guidelines": each contributing student draws whatever images he or she visualizes. These may be words, lists, diagrams or drawings, symbols, or any combination thereof, as long as they indicate the student's understanding of the materials and relationships presented. Thus each student uniquely expresses her or his level of understanding.

As each student presents his or her understanding of the topic, the teacher coaches the class, identifying approaches to consider for extending and refining the topic, as well as means of combining these ideas with those of classmates, using "freewheeling" representations of understanding. Similarities and differences among representations provide opportunities for discussion that lead to synthesis of disparate views. The degree to which consensus is reached is determined by the simplicity or complexity of the topic and the focus for the activity as well as the desired learning outcomes set by the teacher.

As you experience mind mapping with students you will find it is a very exciting form of metacognition, especially for less academically able students. Not only can these students be trained to rely on thinking processes that are natural to them, they also begin to share these processes with classmates. This sharing supports the opening of new modes of thought that can be explored by an entire classroom of students. Because mind maps, in effect, mirror each student's thinking processes, they can also serve effectively as a diagnostic tool for teachers to refer to as they help students focus more clearly on the various aspects in inquiry/discovery. Students who are confused about a given topic find mind mapping a useful means of separating what makes sense from points of confusion. The tool is especially helpful when it is clear to students that further support from the teacher will be forthcoming as a result of their efforts. Further details on the use of this strategy in instruction are available by accessing the Website www.visual-mind.com.

Concept Mapping

Because it calls on students only to write words, concept mapping is a more structured form of mind mapping, used to form a chain of related events or components associated with a given broader (scientific) concept. Concept maps support students as they summarize what they understand about a given concept and its relationship to other apparently similar concepts. In effect, concept maps are useful summaries of what is understood about a given concept. Formalized graphic organizers, such as sequence chains, Venn diagrams, and organizational webs, are examples of concept maps. Because they are a means of organizing information, the development of such student maps can be a useful tool for assessing students' understanding. Developed by students, such maps indicate to teachers (through omissions or misplaced segments) any serious "gaps" in students' understandings of a given concept being studied. Further information about the use of concept maps in instruction is available through www.conceptmap-buysoftware.com.

Supportive Strategies for Students with Special Needs

The question arises, "Is instruction as described in these and other case studies, described throughout this book, appropriate for learning by disabled students and students with special needs?" The answer to this question is definitely yes, as long as teachers offer these students appropriate additional support. Modifications may be required in the equipment that these students would be expected to use in order to be successful learners. In the limited space here it is not possible to develop a detailed account of such modifications. Instead, readers who are responsible for the very important and rewarding assignment of educating these special students are referred to two references that are most supportive. The first of these is *Improving Learning in Science and Basic Skills Among Diverse Student Populations*, Francis X. Sutman and Ana Guzman (1997). (Although the publisher, ERIC Clearinghouse, is no longer supported by the federal government, this publication may still be available by searching the Web, or it can be obtained by contacting fmsutman@msn.com.) Also look for additional, appropriate references listed at the end of the *Improving Learning* monograph. A second reference, *Teaching Chemistry to Students with Disabilities, A Manual for High Schools, Colleges and Graduate Programs* by Dorothy Miner and others (2001), is available through the American Chemical Society. This manual, too, includes many additional sources of information. An additional reference, *Enabled/Disabled: Science Education for an Independent Future* by the American Association for the Advancement of Science (1991), includes a listing of many contacts through which further information and support can be obtained.

Service Learning as an Incentive for Inquiry/Discovery

Too often, a disability of one nature is implicitly assumed to be a general disability. That is not true, as is exemplified in the following narrative.

This example describes the learning of science, technology, and language through photography by twenty severely hearing-impaired beginning high school–age students, who would have been ninth graders but, because of their disabilities, were "enrolled" at the fifth-grade level. They were totally dependent on sign language to communicate with others. At this school, these teenagers were the group that exhibited the most severe behavioral problems, a problem that resulted in part from the fact that they had very low levels of self-esteem and low levels of family support.

Because several of the students had demonstrated interest in an exhibit of photographs displayed in the school, the decision was made by the instructional team and administrator to apply to a local foundation for a small grant to be used to develop and equip a photography darkroom, and to purchase cameras and support equipment, so that the school could offer a course in photography expressly designed for these difficult students. Funding was secured, as was the assistance of two student teachers pursuing careers as special education instructors, under supervision from a faculty member at a local college.

Hands-on instruction began with teaching the students how to use standard cameras. Meanwhile the equipment for the darkroom had been acquired so that the photography group could learn how to develop their pictures and make enlargements. These activities led to instruction about how cameras work, how images of light are chemically imposed on film and printed on paper, and the fixing process. In the course of that instruction, the physics and mathematics skills related to picture enlargement were taught. Finally, the students created posters describing what they had learned.

The activity developed into a service learning experience when the students agreed to record the behind-the-scenes activities of another class, which was transforming an "idea" that they had developed into a play. Those students were making costumes and sets for the play. The photography class took pictures of those activities and presented their pictorial record to the other class on poster board.

The posters, with titles, descriptions, and photographs of the other class written by the photographers, were included in a display on a bulletin board prominently placed near the entrance to the school. Thus the people who attended the performances of the play were able to see how the play was put together behind the scenes. The photography activity had sparked such interest throughout the school that the class organized an assembly program and gave a presentation to the entire student body and teachers, describing what they had learned and displaying images with appropriate captions. In preparation for their presentations, the students had to practice using their pictures while presenting, which spurred them to find appropriate language to express their ideas.

The outcome of this fifteen-week experience was astonishing! According to a school counselor, who monitored the program's progress, the "photography students" overall added two thousand new words to their vocabularies! This is compared with the thirty new words learned by another fifth-grade control group in the same period of time. The envy of the school, even more rewarding for this group of students was the self-esteem of these once "discarded" students skyrocketed as they shared information about their newly developed craft. Not only did these students' attitudes toward learning improve through the photography experience, their behavior also significantly improved. As important as the content learned by both these students and their teachers was the "learning about learning," through involvement in this service activity.

This example of "service learning" instruction can be emulated at all levels of schooling. Its successes indicate that the technique of spurring investigation by triggering the natural curiosity of students requires serious future exploration and adaptation.

Integrating Language Arts and Science: Another Look

The process component of the National Science Education Standards, the practice and development by students of inquiry/discovery skills, is far more likely to be met if it is also considered to be a goal of English-language instruction. Because science teachers must emphasize effective language development, a major goal of the language arts curriculum, it would be efficient for teachers of both subjects to cooperate in planning for and carrying out instruction. Students involved in investigations would learn how to be more precise in their use of language. The plus for the language arts teacher is that students would think, speak, and write better when describing actual experiences that are concrete in nature.

To facilitate such cooperative planning, the strategies included in this chapter have proven to be most helpful in meeting the instructional goals of teachers of both subjects. Logistically, teachers might ask, "How is this cooperative approach possible, when science instruction has the advantage of calling upon thousands of hands-on experiences and formal laboratory facilities to use in driving student inquiry/discovery, while English-language instruction has emphasized written materials?" The answer lies in the following similarity: long before hands-on materials were used in science instruction, philosophers and other scholars relied totally on "the tools" of language (stories, plays, discussions, and so on) to drive the inquiries and discoveries of their students and themselves.

A second condition that supports the instructional relationship between science and language is that, without substantial skill in the use of language, scientists would be unable to effectively carry forward or describe scientific procedures and events, nor would they be able to express their conclusions or discoveries to others for the purpose of verification. A third relationship is that language teachers should be able to call on the content and history of science, as well as other scientific writings and reports, for use in developing the practical language skills that they wish their students to develop. These skills include giving attention to students' oral and written reports of completed investigations and other science experiences. In effect, in the real world, professionals from both fields do depend on one another to meet the demands of their respective professions. Even in school environments this interdependence should be expanded upon.

Using Language Arts Instructional Approaches to Create Science Reports

In large public schools, where students at a particular grade level do not necessarily share the same schedules across subjects, the goal for collaboration can be addressed and met by teachers of science and teachers of other subjects agreeing on experiences to be included in the curriculum. Even if teachers from these disciplines are unable to collaboratively plan and execute lessons, the science teacher may "borrow" valuable preparation and assessment tools for creating reports (rubrics for preparing and assessing science reports are presented in Chapter Seven) from the repertoire of the language arts teacher.

Once students have gathered data or information, it does not become truly synthesized until they can process that information and express it. Over the past twenty years, language teachers have been developing a variety of tools, such as graphic organizers and prewriting strategies, to help their students organize their thinking in preparation for stating what they have learned. See, for example, the "Critical Squares," a prewriting technique, in Appendix B. Although certainly not a new approach, it is particularly valuable because it demands that students focus upon selecting and responding to four of the questions they formulated during the course of their investigation. After brainstorming to identify characteristics to be addressed with the answers to those questions, they would then prioritize the order of the content, either chronologically, perhaps for a lab report, or sequentially, remembering that the strongest information is presented last (where it will have the greatest weight), and the second strongest first, because a strong lead-in involves the reader positively. Then they would write the draft of the report, either individually or as groups (with each member originating a portion of the draft and peer reviewing their segments). That draft would then be self- and peer or parent–reviewed for suggestions for revision. There should be room for additional comments to be made by the teacher if the draft poses special problems for the writer before its completion. Students would review those comments and set goals to be accomplished in the revision. Once the drafting phase has been completed, the student submits the revised final draft to the teacher for response.

A more complex format that works well for developing responses to research activities is presented in Appendix B.2, "The Note Web: Defending Supports for Hypothetical Answers." When using this resource, students identify a key question to initiate an investigation that would require the use of a variety of sources for finding the answers. Then students brainstorm about a range of places to look for those "reliable" sources. Teachers should encourage personal contact (interview or letter of inquiry, for example) as well as use of Websites that provide knowledgeable staff members to answer specific questions. During the investigation, the teacher would review what is meant by "new" information and how to acknowledge the source for each. This becomes a valuable opportunity to teach about plagiarism and careful referencing of information. Furthermore, it serves as an opportunity to remind students that referencing sources is a safeguard for themselves. No one expects them to be experts, but they are expected to be able to find the experts, evaluate the reliability of the information provided, then present sources as backups who can verify the bases for the students' own hypotheses and conclusions.

A particularly helpful tool for developing and assessing understanding is the "letter to a friend" activity demonstrated in Chapter One as a cumulative activity in the "wagon in the hallway" activity. Such an activity provides a framework for a narrative description of the investigation and tests a student's ability to describe what was done and how the findings "fit" that experience.

Once such tools have been gathered, they can be modified to meet the specific needs presented by the activity, for the skills expected of the specific student population, and by what the teacher finds to be most adaptable to his or her needs. For example, in Chapter Seven, Exhibit 7.4, item 5, the general question, "Have you explained how it demonstrates the characteristics expected, or identified problems encountered?" might be modified to address a specific focus expected of the student in the report: application, comparison or contrast, synthesis, or a general summary of what has been gained through the investigation. Or that focus might be added at another point, because in a laboratory report the teacher might wish to also have students explain how what they anticipated experiencing differed from what they actually encountered, as well as describe the quality of learning achieved in the experience itself. Those drafts would then be self- and peer-reviewed (see the rubric in Chapter Seven). Students set goals for revising the work, then use the suggestion made by their "coaches" to develop the revisions. The final draft then would be presented to the teacher for evaluation.

Summary

In summary, this chapter should assist in emphasizing the importance of taking into conscious, serious account the role of language in developing science understandings among science students. The message conveyed here is that much more attention needs to be given to the significant role that language plays in both the development and practice of inquiry/discovery skills. However, the concern alone does not lead to success, especially if it is limited to learning definitions for scientific terms. If science learning and the practice of inquiry/discovery are to be attained at the levels desired, instruction has to go well beyond the memorization level! It is the responsibility of science teachers to address language concerns, especially as students formulate the level of *questions* appropriate to inquiry/discovery. Several appropriate strategies useful in addressing these concerns include peer teaching, the jigsaw approach, brainstorming, hypothesizing, hitchhiking, and mind mapping (or concept mapping). These strategies make that growth occur naturally during the process.

If you as a science teacher are uncomfortable about the significant role language skills play in the development of a successful instructional program, don't hesitate to plan to work with other teachers, especially language teachers. A specific example of the benefits of such collaboration is described in Chapter Four (Lesson 3: Energy Conservation). This cooperation will benefit both you and your students. If such collaboration is not possible, use of the fine tools developed by language arts teachers will assist you as you support your students to effectively develop their language skills.

Chapter 7

Assessment of Inquiry/Discovery and Content Learning

ASSESSMENT CONTINUES to be the most dreaded word in school language. Since the passing of the No Child Left Behind Act, with the accompanying penalties for failure to meet the standards set, the arguments about the format and content of tests, testing procedures, and outcome interpretations have become increasingly vitriolic. In the inquiry/discovery classroom, assessment takes on special meaning because the process is ongoing and measures both content mastery and the level of initiative students attain in directing their own education.

Assessment, especially as it relates to student learning, is of major importance in the inquiry/discovery classroom. It also poses dilemmas. With the federal No Child Left Behind Act now mandating that states implement standards-based testing in science as in mathematics and language arts, along with accompanying penalties for failure to meet the standards, teachers are under more pressure than ever before to prepare students for high-stakes science content tests. Although conventional, standards-based testing has been widely critiqued for its emphasis on factual recall of information over demonstration of upper-level thinking concepts (Bracey, 2005), such forms of assessment are likely to continue at the state and district level. For the teacher involved in inquiry/discovery instruction, the task is to devise assessments that identify students' strengths and weaknesses in both content understanding and skills development and to modify instruction so that students can effectively master the content set forth in state-based science standards as well as the skill-oriented inquiry learning called for in the National Science Education Standards. An additional element is to encourage, and then assess, students' initiative and self-direction in their learning process. In this chapter, we offer a variety of assessment approaches and rubrics to support teachers in accomplishing these goals. Teachers may select and use these tools at their discretion.

Assessment Goals in Inquiry/Discovery Instruction

Assessment of students in inquiry/discovery science classrooms is based to a large extent on the goals of the lesson, which include objectives for both content learning and inquiry/discovery skill development. For general understanding of inquiry learning goals, it may be helpful to review the five essential components of inquiry instruction as described by the National Research Council's publication *Inquiry and the National Science Education Standards* (2000). These components are as follows:

1. *Questioning*—Learners are engaged in science-oriented questions. That is, the learners themselves ask questions directly related to the content being examined and the concepts being developed through that examination.

2. *Observing*—Learners give priority to finding and presenting evidence responding to questions (inquiries) concerning content or concepts.

3. *Reasoning*—Learners themselves directly formulate explanations based on the evidence they gather themselves through either experimentation or research.

4. *Interpreting*—Learners assimilate that knowledge by making connections between those explanations and prior science knowledge.

5. *Evaluating*—Learners communicate and justify the explanations they have found.

Note that this list of characteristics is hierarchical (from 1, the most literal, to 5, the most abstract) in nature, and roughly replicates Bloom's Taxonomy. Thus specific skills such as measuring, manipulating mathematical data (directly or with a calculator or computer), and preparing tables or graphs of data become *tools* (not the focus for instruction) to be used in the process of attaining deeper understanding of science concepts. If we expect students involved in the inquiry/discovery process to behave differently in the classroom, to become both inquirers generating questions and discoverers who find their own answers, we need to employ a variety of appropriate assessments to gauge their instructional needs and accomplishments. Approaches to assessment need to take into account the science content learned and the language and mathematics skills developed, as well as a clear understanding of the data that has actually been collected. These skills are representative of the capabilities expected of those who eventually contribute successfully to the scientific or technological enterprise, and those who are willing to support its development. To better ensure that this goal is met by students calls for a "rubric based" approach to assessing student learning, a process that will enable both teachers and students to keep track of specific expectations within the body of knowledge and performance measured, and to gauge improvements in the development of skills used as well as the increase in scientific knowledge that develops over time. With foresight and care science teachers will be able to devise a variety of assessments (both formal and informal) that will result in a concrete gauge of student growth and achievement. Once again, we are at the apex of a growing awareness that it is not the "body" of knowledge that we must carry around with us; it is the ability to find and respond successfully to that knowledge that must serve the central focus of inquiry/discovery-oriented learning and must become the focus of student assessment as well.

Approaches to Assessment

The approaches to student assessment take three different forms: *formative* (measuring student assumption of responsibility within the inquiry/discovery paradigm), *summative* (measuring student mastery of concepts and skills expected), and *diagnostic* (determining remediation that tudents may need to achieve the expectations set for them). All three types of assessment may be used to give feedback to students and to guide them in their learning. Diagnostic assessment will be covered in more detail later in the chapter. For the purpose of student grading, formative and summative assessment are the most important. Formative assessments are embedded in daily instructional practice and can serve as ongoing evaluations of students' abilities to conduct inquiry/discovery practices as well as their mastery of content. Such assessments can focus on how well students perform particular tasks (posing appropriate inquiries, analyzing findings, presenting oral reports) as well as the quality of particular products (journal notations, preparation of graphs, lab reports, lesson summary reports). For example, in evaluating how well a student performs during a particular lesson sequence, the teacher might focus on the student's ability to

- Develop appropriate questions and inquiries
- Participate in discussion and team activities before, during, and following investigations
- Demonstrate learning as reflected in the data observed or collected and in the nature and quality of the written report of the investigation
- Construct appropriate tables and graphs of data
- Present oral reports as well as written summary reports of conclusions based on analysis of data and evidence, and also to document "discovery" research and/or its applications

Summative assessment of student learning occurs at the termination or completion of a unit of study and might include the following approaches:

- Exit Tickets (short forms filled out in response to summative questions) presented upon "exiting" the room at the end of a lesson.

- Tests or quizzes calling for brief, selected responses (for example, multiple choice) or more extended responses requiring a brief essay.

- Student-constructed written questions with answers to those questions. (This performance-based approach not only assesses content knowledge but also the ability of students to formulate appropriate inquires.) This approach will be addressed in more detail later in the chapter.

The formative templates and other tools included in this chapter are useful for tracking, assessing, and evaluating the student's involvement in inquiry/discovery activities. A general "all purpose" rubric for assessing individual students through all stages of an inquiry/discovery lesson is presented in Exhibit 7.1. This form includes provision for evaluating student participation in lesson activities, from the Pre-Laboratory to Post-Laboratory phases, including, for example, the student's ability to perform mathematical computations (if any), to prepare graphs, and to formulate final summaries and conclusions. The rubric can be adapted for a variety of purposes depending on the complexity or content of a given investigation.

Assessment of Student Participation and Readiness

When evaluating student progress in the inquiry/discovery classroom, the teacher considers two separate aspects: the student's *mastery* of content and procedures and the student's *readiness* to self-initiate activities. Students have always been expected to be compliant. If they merely accept this role, they may never learn how to take ownership as learners. Following the "Instructional Matrix" (Chapter Three), if the teacher accepts the role of "guide," it becomes the teacher's role to mentor students in transition from one level of self-sufficiency to the next. As we now understand, the student's ability to participate in classroom discussion and inquiry activities is especially important. To ensure that students assume this role, the teacher assesses the quality of student questions as well as the responses given (and their frequency) during discussion activities. Because when the purpose is evaluative the assessment is based mostly on teacher observations, a tool for tracking the effectiveness of student participation is essential. Exhibit 7.2 provides such a tool. For example, while students prepare for a laboratory investigation, the teacher records the contributions made by individual team members. As the teacher circulates, observing student interactions with the

EXHIBIT 7.1

Assessment of Student Learning in Inquiry/Discovery Science Investigations.

Student _____ Subject _____ Period _____

Degree of Student Involvement Scale of 1–5: 1 = minimal participation, 5 = strong leadership role	1	2	3	4	5
Pre-Laboratory Activities					
Did the student effectively call on past experiences to design hypotheses?					
Did the student formulate upper-order questions to direct thinking and performance during the laboratory activity?					
Did the student effectively anticipate the procedures to be used to obtain the necessary information from the activity?					
Laboratory Activities					
Did the student help prepare the laboratory equipment for the experiment?					
Did the student help formulate an expected outcome for the activity?					
Did the student demonstrate understanding of the expected content through actively being involved in carrying out the hands-on activity?					
Did the student demonstrate understanding of the expected content with appropriate responses to the activity as it unfolded?					
Did the student collect the data needed to create the laboratory report?					
Did the student participate throughout the activity as a contributing member of the group?					
Post-Laboratory Follow-Up Activities					
Did the student create an appropriate data chart, graph, or other visual?					
Did the student learn how to convert one form of data into another (data to graph to table, for example)?					
Could the student perform the basic required mathematics and obtain correct answers?					
Could the student formulate valid explanations for the outcomes of the activity?					
Did the student recognize apparent anomalies or discrepancies in outcomes?					
Was the student able to explain how such unexpected outcomes occurred?					
Was the student able to assist the group in formulating a conclusion for the activity?					
Did the student actively participate in developing a report describing the activity, its results, and the conclusions drawn?					
Post-Laboratory Extension					
Did the student participate effectively in designing inquiries based on information gathered in the laboratory activity?					
Did the student discover answers to inquiries by searching appropriate references?					
Could the student clearly write and orally present his or her report?					
Overall Evaluation (averaging points, with or without weighting)					

materials and each other, he or she makes "weighted" notations of the quality of student participation. Strong leadership roles merit asterisks (*); quick notations of " + ," "−," and " √ " are made to indicate other levels of participation. In the evaluation of group problems, "?" indicates student or group confusion, while "0" indicates student or group reluctance to engage in the work actively or the lack of observable contributions. Using this descriptive format, the teacher pinpoints behaviors as they relate to expectations, and identifies student responses to the current level of instruction.

Anecdotal comments describe how well students listen and respond to others, develop explanations for ideas suggested, make specific references to investigation details or to the textbook, draw inferences from informational data gathered by the group, and note how well the group functions together. Examining those notations, the teacher formulates specific responses to team performance. While teams compile laboratory reports, the teacher again notes individual performance. Once he or she has that data, the teacher identifies areas in which the entire class needs support, or designs modified activities and devises remediation for individuals or groups needing additional assistance. Note that, to save space, the form (which would be four separate forms, one for each phase of the investigation process) does not provide space for group or individual students' names. The placement of those would be below each set of tasks described as being appropriate.

Using the form, the teacher would then be able to compare and contrast individuals within the team and across the entire class. Thus at each stage of planning for the next series of activities, this becomes a valuable tool for reorganizing student teams to encourage greater balance of participation and cooperation. The efficiency is more probable when the students are regrouped according to their assessment rankings, rather than alphabetically or randomly.

When students successfully initiate activities, the teacher rewards them for their management; however, he or she also supports students who are uncomfortable with the self-initiated procedures. For example, if students balk at the assignment, are unable or unwilling to write questions (inquiries), or are reluctant to self-select reading assignments suggested by peers, the teacher steps in and initiates those steps. Having done that, the teacher identifies the stumbling blocks to self-initiation and modifies expectations, procedures, or both until those students develop the confidence and skills necessary to obtain the next level of independence. Point discussions based on Bloom's Taxonomy (described in Chapter Six) are also helpful as incentives for student participation and rewards for the levels of participation demonstrated.

EXHIBIT 7.2

Rubric for Assessing Lesson Participation Through Observation.

Class: _____ Activity: _____ Date: _____

Pre-Laboratory Activity

Student	Engaged in formulating questions for investigation	Contributed to reading	Participated in discussion	Contributed to developing inquiry	Participated in the discovery process	Actively suggested additional inquiries, research
Group: Students						

Laboratory Activity

Student	Participated in setting up investigation	Identified problems with procedures	Suggested procedural changes	Actively participated in laboratory investigations	Collected data during investigation	Assisted in developing laboratory report format and content
Group: Students						

Post-Laboratory Activity

Student	Participated in reviewing data for accuracy	Identified problems to be described in report	Identified procedural changes to be explained in report	Actively contributed to organization of laboratory report	Organized data for inclusion in laboratory report	Developed a draft of segment of laboratory activity for group review
Group: Students						

Post-Laboratory Extension

Student	Participated in identifying topics to be explored	Assisted in creating relevant questions	Proposed resources to be used to gather information	Actively contributed in finding relevant materials	Organized data for inclusion in summary report	Developed a draft of summary activity for group or class review
Group: Students						

Note: Each of these charts (Pre-Laboratory, Laboratory, and Post-Laboratory, plus Extension) would be separately prepared for the entire class, so that the teacher would not have to keep flipping from chart to chart during class activities.

Assessing Science Investigation Reports (Rubrics)

The science teacher assigns two major kinds of reports: personal investigation reports of laboratory experiences and final "summary" reports (often compiled by groups), analyzing research findings and explaining conclusions. Both are used in assessing content learning, but the differing methods for obtaining the information (firsthand versus reaction to others' experiences) and the different ways students can be expected to assimilate the information gathered are considered when evaluating their presentations. Because report writing is such a significant science classroom activity, it is crucial to find effective ways to generate good reports and assess them. When the opportunity arises, cooperation with a language arts teacher is strongly encouraged. The laboratory report presents the student's findings from an investigation and should clearly explain the topic, the investigative procedure, and the final results, and should draw from mathematical data or other evidence to support any final conclusions. A description of the reasoning or interpretation that leads to the conclusion made, including any further related inquiries to be considered as a result of the findings presented, should also be included. A rubric for assessing written laboratory reports is included as Exhibit 7.3. Although this rubric can be used by the teacher for evaluating either the rough draft or the finalized report, students can also make use of it for evaluating their own work prior to submission to the teacher.

Evaluating written investigative reports using rubrics increases students' comprehension of content expectations as it enhances language development. When the teacher introduces such rubrics, it is best also to offer opportunities for students to ask questions that lead to an understanding of the rubric's function. Later in the science course, students may assist in designing their own rubrics, modeled on those already used. The most effective rubrics provide at least three columns for assessors. The first column is for use by students to assess themselves; the second (optional) is for a peer or parent assessor; and the final column (traditionally on the right) is for the teacher. An example of a rubric for use in such cases is provided as Exhibit 7.4.

When using rubrics in responding to student reports, it is vital for the teacher to include comments indicating where and how the reports are *incomplete* in their responses, and to identify areas where the information is *inaccurate*. When the teacher returns the graded reports to the students with the completed rubric, the rubric serves the student as a guide to self-assessment and revision. Contrasting self-scored points with those

---

EXHIBIT 7.3

Evaluation of Individual Science Investigation Reports.

Student's Name _____

Title of Report _____ First Draft _____ Final Report _____

Writing Goal: To present your findings for the topic above, demonstrating the skills you have used to collect and analyze data, and draw a valid conclusion based on those findings.

Evaluation:

"O" = information missing, "N" = needs improvement, "S" = satisfactory, "E" = excellent

The written report was submitted on time: yes _____ no _____

Evaluation Factors	O	N	S	E
Content:				
Statement of problem or inquiry is addressed.				
Report uses scientific terms accurately.				
Hypothesis, if any, is identified.				
Investigative procedure is clearly described.				
Observations and/or data collected are clearly detailed.				
Report organizes data and other information effectively.				
Mathematical calculations performed, if any, are correct.				
Table, graph, or drawing is adequately prepared and labeled.				
Results are appropriately analyzed, with any anomalies or discrepancies in outcomes identified.				
Conclusions are well formulated, with explanations based on data collected and related supporting evidence.				
Scientific terms are appropriately used and understood.				
References consulted are cited.				
Writing:				
Focuses on assigned topic				
Organizes paragraphs effectively				
Presents clear summary statement				
Uses appropriate grammar including punctuation and spelling				
Uses precise word choices				
Is typed using a computer keyboard				
Other Factors Unique to This Report **Related Inquiries Posed**				

Additional Comments:

awarded by the teacher and reading the teacher's comments help the student as he or she identifies the reasons for the discrepancies. Once students understand what to change, they are allowed to revise *one* segment of the report rather than the whole, to be submitted *with the report rubric* for regrading. Although this practice may generate more work for the teacher,

<u>**EXHIBIT 7.4**</u>

Self- or Peer Evaluation of Science Reports.

Name _____

Title of Report _____

Writing Goal: To present your findings for the topic above, demonstrating the skills you have used to collect and analyze data, and to draw a valid conclusion based upon those findings

Evaluation:

O = missing (0)   I = incomplete or inadequate (5)

N = needs improvement (6)   S = satisfactory (7)

G = good, but needs development (8)   E = excellent (10)

Name of peer/parent evaluator: _____

Specifications **Have you**	Self Peer/Parent	Peer/Parent	Teacher
1. Introduced your topic *adequately*?			
2. Explained the *nature* of your investigation?			
3. Included the information *gathered*?			
4. Detailed *specific* outcomes of the investigation?			
5. Explained how it demonstrates the characteristics expected, or identified problems encountered?			
6. Concluded your topic logically?			
7. Written in complete sentences?			
8. Used correct spelling and punctuation?			

Using the chart above, please assign a "grade" to the paper based on the degree to which each requirement meets expectations. Each number is worth up to 10 points, depending upon point values (given above) for each evaluations.

Score			

Comments:

it is an essential step if the student is to learn how to improve responses on future assignments. Of course, the rubric, comments, and scores guide the teacher in the regrading process. Student grades then are based on the degree to which students improve the report. They quickly learn to select the worst segment and make it into "the best," in order to get more "bang for the buck." Everyone profits from the experience.

Creating and Evaluating Team Reports

In the case of more complex material, or material the entire class is assigned to examine, team reports are an effective approach because students have opportunities to interact, discussing both content for clarification and the most effective ways to present their results. One group report-writing technique is referred to as the "Round Robin" approach. Each member of the team is assigned to write a different section of the report. The entire group reads each segment and edits the contents for clarity and accuracy. The team then selects the most important information from each segment of the report to incorporate in developing the final conclusions. Although one student produces the final written draft resulting from these discussions (for extra credit), both sets of drafts are submitted for the grade. This approach has two merits: first, the students are able to help each other understand the content, and second, the outcome produces fewer reports for the teacher to evaluate. The prior drafts ensure that each student receives credit for developing topics the final report. In addition, reading the rough drafts gives the teacher a gauge of the understanding of each participant, and assists in the evaluation of individual participation in developing the total report. The single final draft allows the teacher to focus attention on the group's final understanding of the content. Exhibit 7.5 clearly demonstrates the differences in purpose and procedures expected from students when engaged in preparing such group reports.

EXHIBIT 7.5

Holistic Evaluation of Group Science Reports.

Content

Requirements (20 points)   Meets expectations:

                                    Supplies appropriate and significant information
                                    Supports conclusions with appropriate documentation

Focus (15 points)   Narrows topics:

                                    Provides specific details, examples, data to demonstrate position
                                    Draws a conclusion

                                    Makes a clear statement of learning gained

                                    Identifies its application to the objective set

Approach

Commitment (15 points)   Uses time productively:

                                    Confers w/self (proofreads and edits), w/peer, w/coach (often, teacher or parent)

                                    Revises draft to reflect influence of conferences

Risk-Taking (10 points)   Tries new modes:

                                    Selects topics, forms, techniques, etc., especially brainstorming, mind- or concept mapping, research, prewriting

---

Performance Tasks: Alternative Content Assessment

As noted in earlier chapters, it is a common practice in inquiry/discovery lessons to encourage students to generate a certain number of questions (or inquiry problems) in writing and respond to them. This task can be introduced at any stage of a lesson, either before or after a laboratory activity, and is often used as an alternative form of content assessment. Unlike conventional test questions, performance activities (including "question generating" exercises) require students to apply what they've learned in the lesson to related situations, and therefore can offer a deeper picture of the student's conceptual understanding and knowledge.

For an example of this type of performance task, we remind you about the "distance from the Earth to the Sun" investigation in Chapter Four. In the original lesson, students were given an assessment task of calculating the distance from the Earth to the Moon using the knowledge and tools gained from the earlier lesson itself. However, the one unknown to be discovered was the *diameter* of the sun. A related assessment task that could be given might be worded as follows:

"Recall how you determined the distance from the Earth to the Sun to be close to 9.3×10^7 miles. On the basis of this knowledge, describe how you could now verify the Sun's *diameter*."

A student might respond as follows:

Draw similar triangles labeling the distances represented by comparable sides of the triangles, allowing X to represent the diameter of the Sun.

$$\frac{\text{Distance from the Sun to pinhole}}{\text{Distance from pinhole to image}} = \frac{\text{Diameter of the Sun } (X)}{\text{Diameter of the Sun's image)}}$$

In this task, students are asked to solve an equation similar to one they solved before by making a different substitution. This enables the teacher to evaluate how well students understand the relationships demonstrated in the "distance from the Earth to the Sun" investigation. If they understand use of simple math to indirectly determine the value of an unknown quantity, they will be able to perform the task successfully.

Hands-on testing and performance assessment are valid and highly appropriate outcomes for inquiry/discovery investigations. The tests themselves can be designed to determine more than can be shown through response to multiple choice or true-false types of test items and offer a far more valid indication of mastery of concepts taught. In Appendix C we offer an excellent resource for developing assessment activities specifically designed to measure what has been learned and to identify the next steps in lesson planning. However, to be appropriate the tasks must be parallel to but not mirrors of activities already performed in class. Because students must be prepared also to respond to paper-and-pencil high-stake tests, they must be afforded opportunities to respond to such tests as part of their experience in the science classroom.

Summative Assessment: Inquiry-Oriented Classroom Tests

Because we often refer to Bloom's Taxonomy (see Exhibit 6.1) for supporting students to think critically in their oral and written discourse, and especially in generating questions, it can also be helpful to make use of the Taxonomy for creating test questions and exercises. Taking into account the three major cognitive levels, tests can be devised that require students not just to *recall* content information but to *analyze* or *evaluate* it. In this way, the tests can examine students' thinking that most closely corresponds to the *reasoning*, *interpreting*, and *evaluating* modes of inquiry mentioned earlier in the chapter. For example, here is how the Bloom cognitive levels might be connected to particular student tasks and testing methods:

1. Knowledge and Comprehension (Factual Recall)

   Task: Students supply scientific definitions, provide explanations, and cite examples.

   Mode: Selected Responses (SR)—Multiple-choice, matching activities, modified true-false

2. Application or Analysis (Compare or Contrast)

   Task: Students are given short reading and are then asked to identify an appropriate hypothesis to fit the facts presented; to draw inferences; to categorize and classify data; and to construct an organizing graphic or to perform other activity that demonstrates their thinking.

   Mode: Brief Constructed Response (BCR)—Sentence completion, short explanatory statements, diagram preparation

3. Synthesis or Evaluation (Problem Solves)

   Task: Students are presented with problems to solve, with complex questions to answer in detail, with scientific findings to interpret or evaluate, or with any activity requiring them to demonstrate skill in seeing relationships or among parts within new information presented or in integrating and synthesizing disparate data.

   Mode: Extended Constructed Response (ECR)—Problems, questions, or tasks requiring essay responses with clear conclusions and examples

When evaluating the content of the test and the testing procedures selected, the judgment should be based on the levels of competence you expect students *in this class* to demonstrate. Make sure these levels are appropriate, both for the skills expected of these specific students and to the "Essential Curriculum" guidelines set by your district or state.

Observation and Diagnostic Assessment

Diagnostic assessment is a powerful tool in a teacher's arsenal. By organizing and prioritizing the observational data, the teacher can form remediation groups and reassign work groups, based on students' strengths and weaknesses. A useful form for this purpose is presented in Butler and McMunn in *A Teacher's Guide to Classroom Assessment*, and is reproduced in Appendix C. This assessment can be used to assist students in achieving mastery as well as to evaluate their current achievements. A flow chart mapping out alternative courses of action depending on student readiness for the next level of independent inquiry might be useful for some aspects of lesson planning in the inquiry/discovery classroom. The key here is the preplanning. The teacher anticipates classmates needing remediation or assistance and prepares in advance for handling groups in "coach" or help-class situations. Ideally these would take place after school when the teacher could give undivided attention to assisting with the work. However, in the real world, these could take place in the classroom while more advanced students are doing independent research (with hardcopy or computer activities). Having those students find materials closely related to current classroom projects, aware that they would present their findings to the entire class, would keep them focused on the task at hand while the remedial groups receive assistance.

The Teacher's Shifting Roles in Inquiry/Discovery Assessment

In the inquiry/discovery classroom, students assume responsibility for their own learning by giving feedback about what they don't know and demonstrating new learning by selecting segments of their reports for revision. This shift in roles for students changes the teacher's role. Traditionally that role has been the "director," who takes full charge and responsibility for directing all aspects of learning. In this situation, the students' responsibility is to respectfully undertake tasks assigned and complete them. They are required to accurately recall what they experience under the teacher's direction. Like the director, the teacher in the new role of "leader" assumes responsibility for fully supervising the learning process, but he or she initiates and supervises instruction while indicating when students are expected to accept responsibility for portions of their own instruction. The teacher, who "guides" students through the learning process, assesses students' readiness for increased independence and encourages them to accept responsibility for additional aspects of their learning, providing the tools for doing so. For example, instead of giving them questions to answer, he or she "steers" them in the direction of formulating inquiries appropriate to the goals established. As a result of observation and assessment, the teacher identifies limited areas in which he or she must take charge, closely monitoring and supervising student progress, and areas in which the students are competent to support their own learning. Finally, the "mentor" functions as an "engaged" observer of the ongoing learning process. He or she assumes the responsibility for measuring student performance, deciding where they have succeeded or need assistance, giving feedback about their progress, and modifying the program approach to better assist them as they inquire about and discover science concepts.

Selecting the appropriate role is an important part of a teacher's assessment responsibility. It must be a match for the teacher's own personality and self-image and must meet the needs of students themselves; the role assumed may vary from class to class depending on the makeup of each. Assessment is the key to deciding when and how to shift from role to role.

Teachers who have never experienced the student inquiry/discovery process in their own classrooms worry that, if the students themselves are performing the learning tasks, the teacher is without a function, except to occasionally interact with them. To visualize a classroom in which the teacher truly functions as a guide and occasional mentor, consider the following scenario.

"Mentored" Biology Lesson (Level 3): Symbiotic or Parasitic Relationships

Pre-Laboratory Activities: A lot of preparation and anticipation of student responses goes into planning successful inquiry/discovery activities in the classroom. In this case, the teacher anticipates that students will be much more likely to be actively involved if presented with evidence (especially if a little bit gross; after all this is middle school) that demands questions as well as answers.

The teacher brings in a tomato leaf upon which a hornworm, infested with the eggs of a parasitic wasp, sits. Without comment she shows the students the exhibit. In the journal they keep for this class she asks them to write three questions they want to see answered about this observed phenomenon. (She asks that they not consult together at this point.) While they are writing, she circulates through the classroom, making notation on a modified class list (Exhibit 7.2: "Rubric for Assessing Lesson Participation Through Observation") of the responses they are making (as to number of questions, and the skill with which they are expressed). Some have no questions; several have more than three. Many are struggling with the wording for the questions they want to ask. She observes some using the "Inference Skills Diagram" (Figure 6.3) provided to help them formulate questions. She makes note of that as well. Then, under her direction, the students compare their questions, and compile a list to be investigated.

The teacher then asks students to describe their reactions to the activity. How hard is it to think of questions? How satisfied are they with the questions they wrote? What problems do they have expressing their questions? What "tools" have they used to help them create questions? During the discussion, they examine their metacognitive processes and identify ways to formulate appropriate questions for investigation. There is a request for vocabulary words to describe the relationship they have observed. She asks students if they can tell whether the relationship is "good" or "bad," and how they "know." Several students "presume" it must be bad, because, as one says, it looks "nasty." She receives a laugh when she asks if that is a scientific judgment, but the question leads students to question how to determine the validity of observations and conclusions. Students propose that they continue to observe the specimen and write reports describing what happens when the eggs hatch.

To prod their thinking, the teacher asks this question: "Is this relationship unique or commonplace in nature?" The students volunteer (for homework) to see if they can find other examples. One student asks if the examples have to be insects. The teacher says no, but that insects will be the focus of the class investigations. Again students ask for vocabulary to describe the insect "relationship" they see. The teacher defers answering that question, pointing out that if it is unique, there probably is no vocabulary, but if it is common, there might be several vocabulary words that would be appropriate, depending on the kinds of relationships seen. As they talk, on the class rubric chart she makes additional notations about the quality of their responses. A student, impatient to begin finding answers, has opened the textbook to the unit on insects and is looking for pictures similar to the infested hornworm. Another student, seeing what he is doing, requests permission to go to the classroom resource center and get a book on insects. The teacher asks the student with the textbook to identify a section he thinks the class should read. Although he has not found precisely what he is looking for, after skimming, he locates a section on habitats, with a special reference to gardens. Other students open books and ask for the page number. The teacher suggests that, before reading, they identify what they hope to find. Once again they are asked to note the questions in their journals. As they formulate questions, the teacher again circulates to note whether the question-making discussion has assisted those having problems with their new assignment. Several appear to have found this task easier. She also notes those who are prereading topic headings and looking at pictures to help them create questions. Once again the class shares their questions and the procedures used to create them. They settle to read, and the teacher takes the opportunity to assist a student who appears to have the greatest difficulty identifying appropriate questions. She makes special note to check with his language arts teacher about reading attack and comprehension skills. She is pleased to note that he too settles in to read, apparently less frustrated than he had been initially by the assignment.

A fast reader has jumped ahead, and found references to symbiotic and parasitic relationships. He beckons her over and asks if these are the vocabulary words they will need. She congratulates him on his inference skills but pledges him to silence. She points out it is more fun to make discoveries for oneself. He shows her his answers to the reading questions and asks permission to go online to investigate the words further. She grants permission as another observant student flips to the appropriate page, finds the same information and asks if they can split the task. The teacher agrees that she may join the other student at the computers, once she has actually finished the reading and answered the questions.

Circulating, the teacher notes students working, and those who lag behind. She responds appropriately, congratulating those on task and gently prodding those who are not. She is careful to note reasons given for not being involved. She compiles a list of those who are unsuccessful and plans to compare it to previous lists. As a follow-up she notes a need for a pair-reading activity for those who do not work well independently. She identifies minimal answers and plans for addressing this performance problem. Meanwhile additional students have found the vocabulary words and are eager to share them with the class.

Pre-Laboratory Activity: At this point, the teacher asks for attention and uses a show of hands to inventory student progress. She is alert to responses that differ from the progress she has noted through observation. She announces the amount of additional reading time remaining before the class moves to a discussion of investigation procedures. As pre-investigation preparation, she asks several important questions before sending them back to work: How will they successfully observe small creatures such as insects? How will they measure and record their observations? What tools will they need to closely observe the insects? Where will they keep those insects so that they can live and be observed? What skills will they need to draw conclusions? In what ways will this activity be like or different from those undertaken in the past? Students note these additional questions in their journals and have time to jot down their initial responses. She reminds them that they should consider any incomplete or unanswered questions part of their homework. (Several wave hands wildly, already picturing some portion of the answers, but she asks them to note their ideas in their journals to be shared later.)

A student asks why the two classmates are at computers. The teacher asks those students to report, describing their progress, providing key words and Website addresses they have used. On a scale of one to five (highest) they identify the usefulness of each site visited. Again students jot down the information in their journals before returning to their own tasks. Before the bell rings the teacher asks students to summarize what they have accomplished, asks what their homework is (also asking if the reading provided suggestions for identifying other symbiotic or parasitical samples), and reminds them that the journals are due at the end of the week. Students tell her what she can expect to see: their homework assignment, proposed questions, answers to the reading questions, and notes about the Websites. As a final point before departure, she asks them to bring in empty liter-size plastic soda bottles with caps and invites them to make hypotheses and diagrams in their journals (before class the next day) about ways the materials can be used.

Laboratory Activities: During the remainder of the unit, in groups, students construct observation stations using plastic window screening and tops and bottoms of the soda bottles to house the insects they collected. Daily they observe (using hand lenses and small microscopes) changes in the relationships among the insects. Using graphic webs they describe characteristics observed in each pair or group; using Venn diagrams they record similarities and differences in relationships between symbiotic and parasitic samples. Their observations and findings are recorded in notebooks left at each station, so that they can read each other's comments and respond to them.

Post-Laboratory Activities: In discussions and reports students compare and contrast their findings with groups studying other examples; they consult with classmates when findings are confusing, then move to classroom and online resources for clarification. Each student selects one example and writes conclusions about what is observed, then refers to online and hardcopy resources to support conclusions. Students use the rubric constructed by the teacher (with their assistance) to self- and peer-evaluate their reports (Exhibit 7.4) before submitting them to the teacher for feedback and grade. Throughout, the teacher monitors their progress using observational checklists, the report forms they complete, peer- and self-assessments of questioning and collecting skills, and group feedback forms (refer back to Exhibit 2.1, "Research Team Feedback Form").

Assessment: As a summative assessment, the teacher constructs a test to determine the extent of each student's content knowledge of insect relationships. It consists of a section of *selected responses* (a thirty-item multiple-choice test, based on their observations and reports) and *constructed responses* (including a modified true-false section, with short paragraph explanations of changes made to make each statement true); a short paragraph response to a reading selection describing symbiosis; and a "letter to a friend" explaining the characteristics of parasitic insects and their effect on their hosts. Following the grading of this test she presents a summary assessment of each student's learning. This includes an overall participation grade for the initial inquiry components (using the observation formative assessments to devise an effort grade); a learning grade based on the laboratory reports of the experiences gained (group and individual); and her observational notes of student effort, involvement in the laboratory experience (each component of those activities, growth and achievement, was weighed separately), and a grade obtained from achievement on the summative assessment. All of the components are used to construct an average for an overall grade.

Using the component factors, the teacher determines that the class has the greatest difficulty organizing and writing answers to the inquiries and organizing the laboratory reports. As new units are developed, she refocuses her rubrics to assess and identify sources of these problems, then helps her students develop those skills. As a result, as the school year progressed, grades for these two components improved immensely. Even more rewarding, these students continued to be eager to come to science class, where they take control of so much of their learning and show such progress.

A Balance of Assessment Practices

As Butler and McMunn point out in their excellent resource, *A Teacher's Guide to Classroom Assessment* (2006), it is the variety of assessments that gives the fullest picture of student achievement. When asked to justify a "score" or grade, the teacher can point to the range of assessment strategies used (such as rubrics, tests, teacher observations, group feedback forms, journal activities, graphic organizers, and written reports). Explaining what each type of assessment reveals about a student's strengths and weaknesses does much to verify the evaluation and identify steps to assist the student's development. For example, the teacher can highlight how the student's ability to participate in initial inquiry components compares with the quality of the lab report produced, how the teacher's observations of the student's involvement in lab experience supports skills assessments, and whether the multiple-choice test items verify other measurements of content learning. It is important to balance assessment outcomes between growth, students' progress toward the goals set in the inquiry/discovery classroom, and their actual mastery of the science concepts taught. This is perhaps the greatest shift in assessment measurement. What Butler and McMunn call "disposition" (comparable to the Dimensions of Learning characteristics #1, "comfort," and #5, "habits of mind," described earlier) is an important factor in measuring a student's success in instruction. Students need support in developing the disposition to learn, and to see education as exciting and rewarding in its own right, rather than a repetitive series of distasteful tasks simply to be completed.

Self-Initiated Assessment

The ultimate goal for an inquiry/discovery classroom teacher of science is for his/her students to assess their own learning, totally outgrowing the need for instructors. Thus, the teacher supports students in learning to teach themselves. To initiate this process, students are invited by the teacher to construct the tools they will need to use in this self-assessment process, suggesting the characteristics a teacher looks for. This occurs as the teacher circulates from student group to student group. Through discussion, the students in each group self select and begin to consider graphics organizers and why particular organizers best suit their needs. This introduction is followed by students' constructing the rubric they will use to evaluate a written assignment or oral report. They can use an earlier prepared rubric as a model to follow as the basis for their new assessment. Once learning objectives for the unit of study have been clearly identified, the students select the scientific knowledge to be assessed and they design questions or activities to use in testing their understanding.

Sentence stems, based on Bloom or referred to in the "Inference Skills Diagram" (Figure 6.3), generate a bank of questions. As these questions are constructed, students "recognize" test items that are similar to those included on previous tests. As they organize these items by difficulty level according to Bloom's "Blooming Verbs" (Exhibit 6.1), they identify the importance of each item to understanding the unit concepts. After they decide on the points assigned to each level of test items, they "pre-take" the test in groups, compiling suggestions for appropriate answers. Throughout, they are replicating the thinking that goes into constructing good summative assessments. Although all students may not have the skills to enjoy these activities, the procedure has the result of making students more careful readers when taking tests. Insecure learners (especially poor or careless readers) are made uncomfortable by these practices, but there are positive outcomes. They demonstrate greater understanding of word attack skills and increased awareness of the multiple parts of many questions. They expend greater effort during tests, and use test-taking strategies such as highlighting and prewriting to improve performance. It is not unusual for a test-wise student to identify a "fine point" and explain how cleverly it asks for certain information. In a world of fine print and fine points, this is an important skill to be developed.

Summary

Continually embedding assessment in instruction, coupled with teachers' self-evaluation of instructional approaches, results in students' improved learning and greater interest in the subject matter. It also results in increased teacher enjoyment of instruction. At the same time, students' scores on high-stakes tests improve without the undue use of instructional time to directly prepare for those tests. Instead, teachers who prepare themselves by carefully analyzing why they emphasize particular approaches to teaching are able to identify approaches that offer both students and teacher opportunities to practice the critical thinking skills so essential for success in today's school environments and rapidly changing workforce. Those students will be given adequate preparation for using skills that become integral components of the scientific enterprise.

Chapter 8

Managing Inquiry/Discovery in the Classroom

THIS CHAPTER offers suggestions for organizing and managing inquiry/ discovery activities in and out of the classroom. Approaches for managing homework assignments are considered along with strategies for promoting optimal student behavior. The later part of the chapter focuses on the necessary laboratory facilities for enabling students to carry out hands-on investigations and includes suggestions for updating equipment and content materials within a modest budget.

Homework

Teachers of science probably do not have to be reminded that today's middle and high school–level students have substantially different behavior patterns and learning expectations than their counterparts had just a generation ago. Today's students are less patient with sitting through a forty-five- or ninety-minute class period listening to teachers' lectures and with completing what they consider to be simply busy work. They respond poorly, if at all, to constant teacher-asked questions about the previous night's homework assignment. In fact, more and more students do not complete such homework assignments unless the teacher collects the evidence of completion and checks it off in his or her grade book. This condition exists mainly because teachers across subjects do not coordinate well in managing out-of-school assignments, and thus students are frequently overloaded with homework. At the same time, students' attention is more directed to using computers for fun, watching television, talking to friends on cell phones, listening to music on iPods, being involved in competitive sports, working part-time, or simply surviving within a complex and busy home and community environment. Extension of the academic component of school life after formal school hours does not hold the primary place that it did during earlier times. This situation will continue to hold true unless teachers within different disciplines cooperate to consciously design instruction so that out-of-school work is more realistically spaced and so that assignments will better motivate students to extend classroom activities into after-school hours.

Out-of-school assignments given by teachers only because they believe in this approach to learning do not lead to desired learning or to the development of effective behavior patterns. In fact, out-of-school assignments or homework better ensure desired learning outcomes only when such assignments are carefully designed to result in substantial meaning to today's students. In support of this conclusion, we need only refer to a report that appeared in the September 2006 issue of *Phi Delta Kappan* magazine, "Abusing Research: The Study of Homework and Other Examples," written by A. Kohn. For both the middle and high school levels, Kohn reports, research indicates there is no significant relationship between the amount of assigned homework and test scores across subjects. And there is only a slight positive relationship between grades received by students and the amount of homework completed. Kohn is quoted in an editorial in *Time* magazine, "The Myth About Homework" (Wallace, 2006), as follows: "Homework...may be the single most reliable extinguisher of the flame of curiosity."

Teachers of science will best support students addressing and meeting content standards, but especially process skills goals, by making certain that they have ample opportunities to practice these skills. To support this practice to the maximum, both out-of-school and in-school assignments must be carefully aligned with classroom activities as they arise. Assignments lack significance when they are presented hastily and out of context at the end of a class period as students are preparing to leave for their next class. Presenting in this way, as an afterthought, results in little meaning to students. This is because it appears to them that such assignments also have little significance to the teacher. Instead of offering the same out-of-school assignment to every student, we have had success in assigning different out-of-school assignments to different groups of students to be accomplished by interacting through e-mail, and expecting each group to present their results, or information learned, to the remainder of the class. Accomplish this by setting aside a few minutes at the beginning of a class session, prior to the "homework's" completion date, for each student group to organize how it will make its presentation. Allow time, during each presentation, for the class members to raise appropriate inquiries. The teacher then has the option to decide to add additional information or details to the students' presentations, inquiries, and discoveries.

Classroom Management

Students often complain that current educational approaches fail to give them sufficient opportunities to address issues that have significance to them personally or that are critical to today's world. In maintaining discipline in the science classroom, our primary consideration should be less on enforcement of behavior and more on positive ways of involving students in the instructional process. As V. F. and L. S. Jones state in their book *Comprehensive Classroom Management* (1998), "Emphasizing the problem solving approach to instruction results in substantially reduced discipline problems by students." We need only define problem solving as: designing instruction so that students are offered ample opportunities to practice and develop inquiry/discovery skills, with the caveat that these opportunities are carefully designed to address and eventually meet realistic and desirable goals set by teachers or by both students and their teachers working together. With well-thought-through approaches, these goals can incorporate both national and state process-and-content standards.

Success and Feedback: Learning is most effective when instruction is designed so that students have ample opportunities to experience success in learning and when there is reasonably immediate teacher feedback offered on their successes. Understanding needs to be shown when the learning results do not occur as expected. Be especially sensitive to this need, early in the school year, as students adjust to the inquiry/discovery emphasis and to unfamiliar content. Students may benefit from being reminded now and then that although the practice of inquiry/discovery may at first be somewhat confusing to them, eventually the results will become more meaningful.

Basic Skills Enhancement: Learning is most effective when teachers allocate sufficient instructional time to ensure that their students also enhance their basic mathematics and language skills, through science-oriented activities. This does not merely mean grading written and oral reports and solved mathematical problems. Instead it means taking into account the accurate use of these skills during all of instruction, not simply when the time comes to grade student work. At one time, the need for emphasizing correct basic skills was considered appropriate only for English language learners (ELL students). This need, today, has also become prominent even among college preparatory English-language-speaking students. Perhaps this change in need among an expanding student population is, in part, due to students' increase in dependence upon the use of computers. Experience indicates, however, that the need also emanates from too little time being available to learn too many things. How well students learn is not enhanced by an overcrowded curriculum! Designing instruction to ensure appropriate language and math skills usage in some instruction actually reduces the "density" of science content presentation.

Student Contracts: For those few students who do not respond as positively to the instructional strategies above as teachers of science would hope for, or who have other special needs to be met, consider using a "written contract for success in learning science" following the example included in Exhibit 8.1. Note that this sample contract includes opportunity for the student to indicate how the teacher can be of special support to his or her learning. The contract also indicates space for the student to list what he or she is to accomplish in order to benefit from the teacher's support. In addition, there is space to record to whom the student will report the progress being made and when the report will be reviewed. Most important is space set aside for the student, with the teacher's support, to indicate when the level of success is expected to be achieved.

Student Self-Analysis: Exhibit 8.2 is a second form, the "Student Self-Analysis Form," which is designed for use by students (in some cases

---

EXHIBIT 8.1

Sample Contract for Success in Learning Science.

I, _____, do want to succeed in _____
                    (student's name)   (teacher's name)

science class. He/she cares about my success and has agreed to help me in the following ways:

A. _____

B. _____

C. _____

What I will need to do to help out is:

A. _____

B. _____

C. _____

and I will examine my progress and share it with my parents/guardian and _____

on _____.   (other support person)
                    (date or dates)

I will know that I have been successful when _____

_____.

Signed: _____   _____   _____
              (student)   (teacher)   (other support person)

Date: _____

   Source: This form is a variation of one included on p. 199 of V. F. Jones and L. S. Jones, *Comprehensive Classroom Management*, 5th ed., (Boston: Allyn and Bacon, 1998).

gifted students) who require special support in completing laboratory investigations by themselves or within groups. This form can be used as is, or can serve as an example to follow. It may require some modification by teachers who decide the need for use of this strategy. When completed, the form is reviewed by the teacher along with a laboratory report claimed by the student to be completed. Notice that the "form" calls for a written report of each investigation and the discussion resulting from the investigation that has been conducted by the group of students who cooperated in the investigation. The teacher may initially assist each student he or she deems should complete it. Eventually the student should be expected to complete the form by him- or herself.

EXHIBIT 8.2

Student Self-Analysis Form.

Student's Name _____   Science Period _____

Date _____   Responsibility _____   Team Number _____

Title of Investigation _____

Teacher _____   Student's Signature _____

Please use this form to help you to think about and to analyze the effectiveness of your participation in each laboratory investigation. To help you to do this, check yes or no next to each question. Then score "1" point for each yes response.

Question	Yes	No
Do you understand the nature of the investigation?		
Do you understand the reason for being involved in the investigation?		
Did you work with other students to better understand the directions to be followed?		
Did you follow the directions carefully?		
Did you support other team members as needed?		
Did you carefully listen to explanations by others?		
Did you carefully give explanations as needed?		
Did you follow safety regulations?		
Were you respectful of other team members?		
Did you participate in discussion following completion of the investigation?		
Did you develop a complete written laboratory report?		

Use the following scale to determine the grade you earned for being involved in this laboratory investigation:

10 yes responses: A

9–7 yes responses: B

6–5 yes responses: C

Keep working toward obtaining a rating of 10 or A!

Investigation Records: It goes without saying that, as scientists do, each student should be responsible to keep a record of his or her involvement in each investigation in a bound or spiral laboratory notebook. This notebook should include a calendar on which the student writes in due dates for assignments and other information. All notebooks need to include a written or typed list of procedures that students will follow to ensure their safety in the laboratory setting, as well as ensuring maximum learning of both content and process skills. The best results are obtained when students write or type this list as the teacher indicates each required procedure and the reason for its inclusion. It is also helpful to have a duplicate list of rules to follow printed in large letters posted on the classroom wall for immediate reference if needed.

Classroom Laboratory Essentials

To ensure maximum flexibility and safety, space needs to be made available within the science classroom so that overcrowding does not exist. Most state departments of education and other appropriate agencies specify the minimum area of floor space required per student in order to meet safety requirements. Classrooms designed to include tables on which laboratory investigations are to be carried out by groups of students is the ideal arrangement. Until this arrangement is feasible, groups of moveable desks can be placed together to form "laboratory work space."

Cabinets and Shelves: Classroom-laboratory arrangements need to allow space for cabinets or shelves in which to store equipment and materials as well as space for housing cataloged references for use by both students and teachers. One cabinet should be fireproof, and cabinets that contain flammable or other dangerous substances should be kept locked to ensure maximum safety. A large cart with wheels is essential for holding together and moving the materials for use during each investigation.

Various Wall Boards and Demonstration Table: The room should include a sizeable chalkboard or whiteboard and a demonstration table that is not placed in front of the chalkboard. This arrangement allows maximum visibility for students of projected or written material placed on the board. Also needed is a sizeable corkboard for posting inquiries, articles, and student work.

Computers: Several computers connected to the Internet are a must for effective science instruction today. However, there are disadvantages that can accrue from every student having access to his or her own computer. These disadvantages include computer misuse, undue expensive upkeep, and loss of space to carry out real-time basic instructional activity. The availability of individual laptop computers has proven to result in undue expensive repair costs as well as ineffective instructional practices.

Water, Heat, Refrigeration: Sources of water and heat, as well as a refrigerator, are a must. A large sink with running hot and cold water for use in washing glassware and other utensils is a must.

Exits, Other Safety Needs: Science classrooms designed to hold twenty-five or thirty students should have two exit doors for safety. And if your instruction requires the use of chemicals, an eye-wash is a must. For further information about meeting safety and other needs during science instruction, readers are referred to the article "Safe Science Facilities" by J. Texley (2005).

Television, CDs: The availability of television in the science classroom requires special consideration. Because virtually every student has TV available at home, there usually is little need to spend valuable class time learning how to watch TV. Of course there are exceptions to this statement. At times, a program presented on TV can serve as an excellent summary to a unit of study. Films on nature, astronomy, how things work, and certain other Science Channel presentations are examples of useful resources. The negative side of depending on these resources is that use of TV too often becomes an easy way to bypass the need for students to directly experience inquiry/discovery in instruction through hands-on experiences. It is too easy to become too dependent on TV as a major source of information. If used in instruction, care must be made not to "abuse" this form of "lecturing."

Alternative Space and Materials

Limited space and lack of facilities is too often used as reason not to involve students in hands-on inquiry/discovery experiences. This should not be the case, because as indicated throughout this book, it is possible to conduct many investigations using simpler, less expensive materials and to work outside the traditional classroom environment. As indicated in an earlier chapter, use of simpler "everyday" materials from time to time allows instruction to emphasize the concept(s) being addressed rather than place undue emphasis on learning how to manipulate less familiar scientific equipment. In addition to the sample investigations included herein, examples of investigations that call on simpler materials can be found in issues of magazines such as *The Science Teacher*, *Science and Children*, and the *Journal of College Science Teaching*. These all are published by the National Science Teachers Association.

A word of caution, however: science teachers do not want to limit hands-on investigations *only* to simpler everyday equipment and supplies, because this practice, if overdone, cheats students from learning about examples of more recent marvelous available technical equipment and materials that are being used by scientists in their inquiry/discovery efforts. This statement reminds us of one incident when a group of students were denied admission to a "pre-med" program at the college level because they had had no experience during their high school biology using compound or binocular dissecting microscopes!

Persistence: Beginning teachers of science, in particular, should not become frustrated with a perceived lack of adequate space or budget. Instead, they should keep persistently working toward obtaining the space and materials that professional training and experience indicate are required in order to ensure that students have ample opportunities to become involved in instruction that emphasizes effective inquiry/discovery hands-on science experiences. As newer teachers of science continue to learn and develop professionally, their demands for instructional space and materials for use by students undoubtedly will increase. If for no other reason, you will want to continually read scientific journals and science education journals; attend science or science education conferences that also include exhibits of scientific books, equipment, and supplies; and interact with experienced master teachers who have extensive background using such resources.

Clearly, priority needs to be placed on the safety of students and teachers. Yet today's school environment causes too many science teachers to be unduly or overly concerned with safety. It has become an excuse for depriving students of rich hands-on experiences. This leads to weakening instruction and learning as well as reduced motivation to pursue further science training and education.

Computer Simulations: Some teachers argue that simulating laboratory investigations through the use of computers is an effective substitute for the real experience. An example of such a simulated-virtual instructional program has been developed by David Yaron of Carnegie Mellon's Department of Chemistry. It can be observed through www.chemcollective.org. Extensive research, however, through the Center for Science Laboratory Studies (CSLS) has indicated that without a critical mass of real science laboratory experiences, students do not learn either content or process skills to the same level that they will from real-life science experiences. This does not imply, however, that experiences with simulations are not valuable. However, teachers of science must be reminded that there is responsibility on their part to call on their professional judgments to determine when the critical mass of real laboratory experiences has occurred, so that students are ready to benefit from computer-simulated experiences.

Linking Equipment to Lesson Objectives: In deciding on whether to use traditional equipment, micro-equipment, or simulations, teachers need to take into account their instructional objectives, whether the priority for student learning is on developing higher-order thinking (process skills) or learning how to manipulate specific scientific equipment. Although both objectives are important, especially when considering motivating students to pursue scientific careers, the priority must first be on meeting the former objective. This advice is based on the fact that *all* of your science students are being prepared to understand how scientists address issues facing mankind and why they do so. At the same time, it is clear that only 5 to 8 percent of high school graduates will eventually continue studies required to become scientific specialists, and will eventually use the most modern up-to-date scientific equipment. That is, although there is the demand to increase this percentage, say, to 10 percent, the remaining 90 percent of your students require experiences that will prepare them to understand the need for continued support of the nation's scientific enterprise and prepare them to become scientifically literate enough to be able to communicate with others about scientific issues.

In cases in which instructional objectives call for the use of hands-on equipment and that equipment is outdated or not in working order, do not pout about this condition. Pouting teachers quickly cause students to mimic this behavior. And the result is diminished learning. Instead, over time, work toward correcting the perceived deficit(s). Keep in mind that teaching science is a long-term, full-career commitment that can, and will, improve in quality each and every year, if you make this commitment one of your major professional goals. Next year should always be more fulfilling than the present one!

Updating Content Materials: There are various ways of extending available budgets for updating instructional resources. Teachers of science who are proactive in securing adequate instructional materials usually are the ones who receive the most positive responses from their budget-unit heads. Requests for instructional budgets that are thoughtfully and carefully defended also receive higher priority. For example, when considering the expense of printed texts, justify your request for replacement on the need for more appropriate readability levels rather than on up-to-date content or applications of scientific theories. In place of frequently purchasing overly expensive textbooks to update content, the updating can occur by depending on current journals, magazine articles, and Websites. An active student inquiry/discovery instructional environment is exemplified by both teacher and students being involved in the search for materials that lead to the discovery of current or updated information.

Newspaper articles are an inexpensive source of updated content. We ran across a prime example of this in a recent issue of a regional newspaper. The article, on page 2 of the paper, reported on the planarian flatworm being used by scientists to study how stem cells can result in regenerating living tissues and organs. High school–level biology textbooks often refer to the planarian flatworm. However, the application of its regeneration to stem cell behavior will not reach beginning-level biology or life science textbooks for some years, if ever. Teachers of biological sciences are aware that students can observe cut planaria regenerating into totally complete organisms! But how does this happen? And can its study lead scientists to better understand the function of stem cells? Appendix A includes several other examples of such updating supplemental material.

Readers who are not familiar with the concept of "readability levels" as one basis for selecting texts and other print materials can find information about this very useful concept through various Websites. For example, simply referring to "readability formula," "Fry readability formula," or "Dale-Chall formula" in a search engine will lead to ample information.

Purchasing Equipment: Being judicious with your instructional budget may allow you to think about purchasing some "unique" yet more expensive equipment. Yet you may have to justify such costly items. One way to accomplish this is to use the following procedure. Suppose you are considering purchasing a $1,000.00 sensitive electronic balance or a special high-powered microscope or telescope. To justify such an expenditure to your budget unit head, indicate the unit cost per student use. For example, suppose one hundred students will use the desired item five times each year over a period of ten years. This means that the cost per unit of student use would be: $1,000.00 divided by $100 \times 5 \times 10$ student uses, or $0.20 per student use, a modest expense!

If questions should arise about your proposed budget, invite your budget unit head to visit one or more of your laboratory inquiry/discovery instructional sessions with a lesson plan in hand. Indicate, following this observation, how instruction and learning would have been enhanced if you had available the desired equipment.

You, of course, will want to share equipment and supplies with colleagues, both within your school building and perhaps even in neighboring schools. If you do borrow equipment from elsewhere, inform your budget unit head and invite him or her to observe an instructional session in which such equipment is being used by "our students." Hopefully, such an experience will lead to you having your own equipment the following year. One final suggestion: keep an ongoing list of desired or justified equipment and materials that can be quickly referred to should a last-minute budget surplus develop.

Putting It All Together

It is helpful, especially for novice teachers of science, to realize that not all of the pieces may come together at the first trial. The process of planning for instruction that is inquiry/discovery-oriented continues, as noted earlier, to develop over each science teacher's professional lifetime. Keep in mind how fortunate it is that you are a member of the science teaching profession at a time when once again high priority is placed on this component of school instruction. The nation needs you, the community needs you, and the school district will honor your expertise. Every active member of the science teaching profession enters it at different levels of content and pedagogical expertise. Your dedication to the profession and to your students and their futures will enable you to continue to develop to be a master teacher whom students will not forget over their lifetimes.

You will cooperate with teachers of other subjects, but you especially will form alliances with other science teachers and hopefully as well with scientists and basic skills teachers. Keep in mind that we benefit, as do our students, when we realize how fortunate we are to have scientific equipment and supplies as resources to call upon to enhance our teaching with its emphasis on processes associated with inquiry/discovery skills development. Keeping these thoughts in mind, we now turn our attention to the final chapter, "Looking to the Future."

Chapter 9

Looking to the Future: The Globalization Challenge

NOW THAT YOU HAVE COMPLETED READING *The Science Quest*, perhaps you have begun to think about how you plan to enhance your science instruction so that it results in improved learning by your students and prepares them more effectively to enter the nation's workforce. Right from the start, it is hoped that you realize that enhancing instruction, though it begins at a given point in time, will be a professional lifetime project, each year producing better learning results than the year before. As you plan, it is important to keep in mind that adequately preparing your students to be able to contribute effectively to their own personal goals and those of the nation for the twenty-first century are not the same as they were for the twentieth century. In the previous century, the United States was a recognized leader in the industrial world, and its education system was considered "world class," at least until the final decades. Today, we are in the midst of a global economy in which larger nations such as China and India are rapidly catching up to our earlier superiority in terms of technological developments and in the method of education that is preparing their students to contribute to the technological advancement and standard of living of their citizens. We can no longer take our education system for granted, especially in mathematics and the sciences.

Support for Dedicated Teachers of Science

Although the challenges ahead are considerable, this is an exciting time to be teaching science, or to be entering the science-teaching profession, because there are encouraging signs of renewed leadership and initiative across the country to increase public funding and support for educational reforms. A few examples of recent organizational actions of most relevance to science teaching are described in the following text. These examples

175

represent only the "tip of the iceberg" when it comes to support for science teachers' efforts in the years ahead.

• In the year 2000, the U.S. Congress passed the "No Child Left Behind" (NCLB) Act, which mandates that each state implement a process for assessing student learning in the "basic" skills of language arts and mathematics and to use the results of those assessments to improve instruction in these subjects. Beginning in 2007, science was added to the content areas to be assessed. Federal funding to schools is now tied to the results of these state-designed and administered tests. Although there continues to be considerable controversy over the NCLB legislation, the intent is for this testing to result in improved learning in the now *three* basic skills. A major concern regarding the current approach to standardized testing mandated by the NCLB legislation is that the means of assessment, in most instances, is not appropriate for the desired approach to instruction, an issue that has been addressed earlier in this book. It is hoped that the limitations of conventional testing will be recognized, eventually leading to changes in state-based approaches to assessing student learning, especially if teachers, through their professional organizations, insist on such change and help to make it happen.

• To support the movement toward reform in science instruction, the American Association for the Advancement of Science (AAAS) in April of 2007 announced that it had joined forces with the National School Boards Association (NSBA) in launching a project to make available to local school boards advice and resources for improving science-related educational experiences. As noted in *Science*, April 17, 2007, this project is being designed to develop expertise and training for school board members so that they will be able to meet the unprecedented challenges in preparing teachers of science to instruct students in both science and mathematics in ways that respond effectively to the demands of the twenty-first-century global economy. The collaboration announcement was accompanied by the following statement: "While school officials and business leaders see a critical need for improved science, mathematics and technology education in order to close the *urgency gap*, students and their parents remain complacent … helping to close this gap. To eliminate the complacency will be one of the central goals in the historic new collaboration between AAAS and the National School Boards Association (NSBA)."

• Another important report is "An American Imperative: Transforming the Recruitment, Retention and Renewal of Our Nation's Mathematics and Science Teaching Workforce," June 13, 2007. Issued by the Business Higher Education Forum (BHEF), an organization comprising Fortune

500 CEOs, university presidents, and foundation executives, the report describes a comprehensive plan of action to elevate the status of the teaching profession by transforming three key components that would support a more robust world-class teaching workforce. This plan identifies bold strategies to encourage talented individuals to become teachers, and differential pay for higher-demand teachers of subject areas such as science and mathematics. The report is posted at www.bhef.com.

Concluding Thought

We could offer many more examples of concerns for America's future, such as the recent report *Tough Choices or Tough Times*, issued by the New Commission on the Skills of the American Workforce (National Center on Education and the Economy, 2006). However, if we are to create the future that we need, it is important that we reacquaint our students with the spirit of scientific inquiry and discovery that this country was once known for. Bono, of U-2 fame, said it well. In an appeal presented in his editorial, "This Generation's Moon Shot," in the November 7, 2005, issue of *Time* magazine, he described how he as a youngster growing up in Ireland saw America as a place that had infinite possibilities—doing things that most people said were impossible. He saw, for example, that America went to the moon; not just because it was a scientific milestone—a career move for the human race—but also because it was an adventure! He went on to say, "More than ever America needs to review its sense of purpose. Beyond the Moon Shot, America, for example, can defeat disease, humanity's oldest enemy." Of course, we know that this goal cannot be realized unless we, as a nation, are able to prepare an array of appropriately educated and trained scientists and engineers who are backed by a knowledgeable citizenry, including well-prepared and dedicated teachers, especially teachers of science.

To echo the wisdom articulated by Lynn Margulis in Chapter One, we turn to former Vice President Al Gore. In his 2007 book *The Assault on Reason*, he concludes that the need to search for and to share truth is critical to the future well being of our nation. It is important for every citizen to be educated to overcome disinterest in the processes by which we determine what is true and what is false. That process Gore refers to as "fact-based reasoning." We have referred to it, within the context of science instruction, as "inquiry/discovery." The message to schools and to the nation is clear. We as teachers, especially of science, are obligated to prepare ourselves to more effectively involve our students in the practice of inquiry/discovery, preparing them and us to become stewards of the kind of open but informed discussion that will eventually lead all of us not only to become interested in science-related careers or to become supporters of those who do elect this option in an open society, but also to apply the inquiry/discovery processes to the resolution of the many critical issues that our nation already faces and will continue to face in the years ahead. As teachers of science, this must be our primary mission!

Appendix A

Selected Classroom Resources

THE FOLLOWING lists offer selected examples of the many thousands of resources that are available to complement investigations that serve as the driving force in inquiry/discovery-oriented science instruction. The lists include major professional and educational organizations offering science-related journals and other resources. In addition, they highlight basic reference materials, Websites, and other resources that are helpful to the science classroom. Although the journals and some magazines can be obtained through membership in appropriate professional organizations or by direct subscription, they can also be ordered directly by your school or local town library.

Professional and Educational Organization Publications

- *The American Biology Teacher* is the journal of the National Association of Biology Teachers (NABT). More information is available through the NABT Reston office: 12030 Sunrise Valley Dr., Suite 110, Reston, VA 20131-3409 or telephone 1-703-264-9696, or through Website www.nabt.org.

- *Chemical and Engineering News (C&EN)*, as well as many other publications, is available through the American Chemical Society (ACS). For information contact: www.acs.org (1155 16th St. NW, Washington, DC 20036 or telephone 1-800-227-5558).

- *Journal of Chemical Education* and other publications are published by the Division of Chemical Education of the American Chemical Society. Membership in this Division is separate from membership in the ACS. For information see Website www.JCE.DIVCHED.org.

- *Journal of Geoscience Education* is published by the National Association of Geoscience Teachers (NAGT). For further information contact the NAGT office, 31 Crestview Drive, Napa, CA, 94558 or e-mail nagt@gordoavalley.com, or telephone 1-707-427-8864.

- *Journal of Research in Science Teaching (JRST)* reports documented research related to the improvement of science teaching at all instructional levels. For information contact the National Association of Research in Science Teaching (NARST), www.narst.org (12100 Sunset Hill Road, Suite 130, Reston VA 20190; e-mail: info@narst.com).

- *Physics Teacher* is published by the American Association of Physics Teachers (AAPT). More information is available through Sina Kiniseley, AAPT Director of Communications, AAPT, One Physics Ellipse, College Park, MD 20740-3845, or telephone 1-301-209-3322, or through Website www.aapt.org.

- *Science*, the weekly journal of the American Association for the Advancement of Science (AAAS), includes articles on subjects across the sciences; issues from 1880 through the present are available. For information contact: www.aaas.org (P.O. Box 1810, Danbury, CT 06813-9764; 1-202-325-6672). The AAAS administers Project 2061, a long-term initiative to advance literacy in science, mathematics, and technology.

- *The Science Teacher, Science and Children, Science Scope*, and *Journal of College Science Teaching*, as well as other resources, are available through membership in the National Science Teachers Association (NSTA). For information contact: www.nsta.org (1840 Wilson Blvd., Arlington, VA 22201-3000 or telephone 1-703-243-7000).

Magazines and Newsletters

- *Discover Magazine* covers science and technology news (www.discovermagazine.com).

- *National Geographic* (magazine) is published by the National Geographic Society (www.nationalgeographic.com).

- *Natural History* (magazine), published by the American Museum of Natural History, is available through both membership (www.mnah.org) and subscription (www.naturalhistorymag.com).

- *Science News for Kids* (www.sciencenewsforkids.org).

- *Science News Online* (www.sciencenews.org).

- *Scientific American*. For subscriptions see www.scientificamerican.com. For online news, resources, and bookstore see www.sciam.com.

- *Smithsonian* (magazine) is published by the Smithsonian Institution. Further information is available online at www.smithsonian.com.

Basic References and Sourcebooks

- Facts-on-File (Diagram Group): *Biology Handbook, Chemistry Handbook, Earth Science Handbook, Physics Handbook.* Available through online and local bookstores.

- *Handbook of Chemistry and Physics*, David R. Lide. 88th edition will be available 2008–2009. Chemical Rubber Company Press, Taylor and Francis Group, 6000 Broken Sound Parkway NW, Suite 300, Boca Raton, FL 33487-2742. Also available through Scientific American Books (www.sciam.com) and via online bookstores.

- *Milestones of Science: The History of Human Kind's Greatest Ideas*, Curt Suplee. National Geographic Society, 2000. Available through online or local bookstores.

- *Theories for Everything: An Illustrated History of Science*, John Langone et al. National Geographic Society, 2006. Available through online or local bookstores.

Digital Resources

- *The National Science Digital Library (NSDL)* is an evolving resource that brings together all kinds of monitored resources related to scientific and mathematics research and education. This resource is funded through the National Science Foundation, and, for science educators, it offers an ever-growing source of accurate, appropriate, and relevant information. There is a special source of information for K–12 teachers and their students. For more information see www.nsdl.org or call 1-803-497-2940.

- *Public Library of Science* (www.plos.org). This is an organization of scientists and physicians who provide monitored access to free scientific resources for educational use.

General Periodicals

- Newspapers: Most major daily newspapers such as *The New York Times*, *The Los Angeles Times*, and *The Philadelphia Inquirer* include articles about scientific discoveries and events at least on a weekly basis.

- *Time* (magazine) and *Newsweek* (magazine) both often include up-to-date science articles; see www.time.com and www.newsweek.com.

Science Museums

- Museums of science and science centers are located in numerous communities across the country and frequently produce quality science materials at a reasonable cost. For links to the center nearest you, contact the Association of Science Technology Centers (www.astc.org) or call 1-202-283-7200.

Television Programs

- *Nova, Nova Now, Nature, The Planets*, and specials about specific geographic areas of scientific interest, such as *Galapagos*, are scheduled on PBS, Science Channel, National Geographic Channel, and the *New York Times* Channel. (A word of caution: Although these presentations are excellent science, teachers are reminded not to substitute these presentations for hands-on investigative experiences. They should serve as follow-through experiences beyond those experiences in the science laboratory environment).

Appendix B
Writing Tools

APPENDIX B.1
Prewriting Critical Squares Grid.

FIGURE B.1

Topic: ______________________________

Focus for examination and explanation: ______________________________

Directions: Below each key question for this topic, make note of your responses.

Question: ______________	Question: ______________
Question: ______________	**Question:** ______________

Conclusion (with reasons to support it): ______________________________

APPENDIX B.2

The Note Web: Defending Supports for Hypothetical Answers.

FIGURE B.2

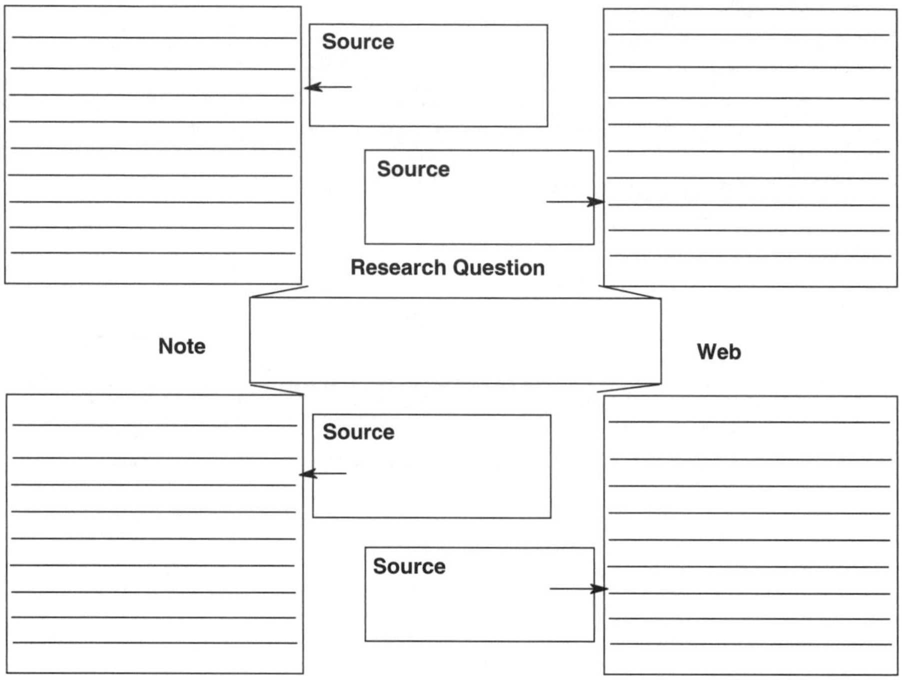

Directions:
1. In each note above, **highlight the information *most specifically* pertinent** to the research/inquiry question addressed here.

On the back of the sheet,

2. State your hypothetical answer to the research/inquiry question.
3. Label each notation by its source, and describe how it contributes to your answer.

Appendix C

Assessment Tools

APPENDIX C.1

Identifying Appropriate Assessment Tasks.

FIGURE C.1

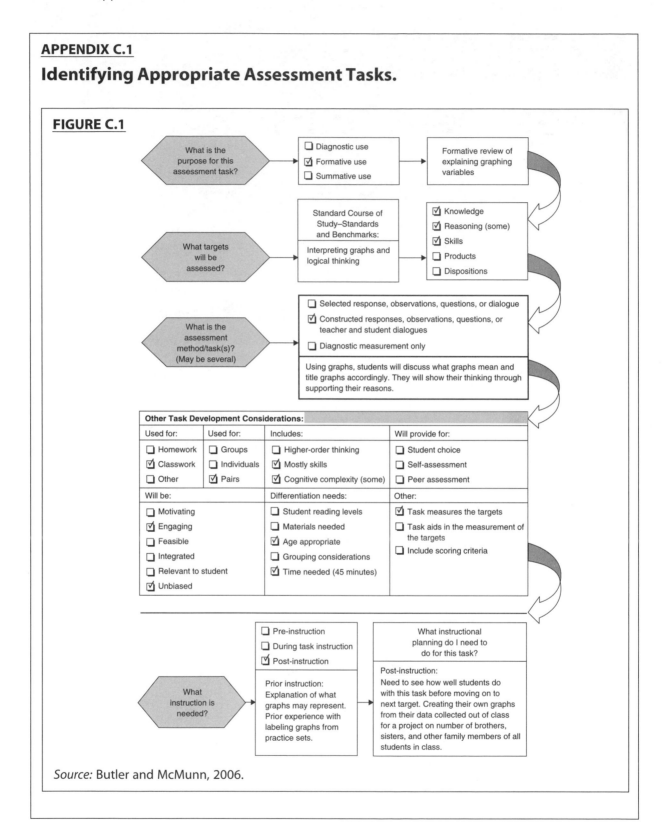

Source: Butler and McMunn, 2006.

APPENDIX C.2

Diagnostic Tool for Creating Remediation Groups.

FIGURE C.2

Example: Science Observational Tool—Preassessing Measurement Skills

Science Class: Period 4

Targets (GH = groupings for additional help on selected targets)

| | GH-A | | | | GH-B | | GH-C | | | GH-D |
	Making Comparisons	Unit Understanding	Unit Use	Unit Conversions	Data Organization	Graphing	Mass	Density	Weight	Measurement Tools
Michael	√	√	√	No	√	√	?	?	?	No
Michael does not understand M, D, and W relationships and how to use science tools. Michael needs to work with Groups D, C, and A when I cover these relationships again.										
Sam	√	√	√	√	?	No	√	√	√	√
Sam has limited knowledge of taking data from a table and making a graph. Needs practice. Will give Sam some graphing activities for homework to work on. Attend Group B session.										
Terry	√	√	√	√	√	√	√	√	√	√
Terry can move on with mass, density, and weight lab.										
Donnie	Yes	No	No	No	—	—	—	—	—	—
Donnie will join Sandy, Bryan, Lakisha, and me in Group A on units. He also needs to join Group C and D sessions on mass, density, weight, and tools.										
Caroline	√	√	?	?	√	√	?	?	?	No

Source: Butler and McMunn, 2006.

References

Alberts, B. "Foreword." In National Research Council, *Inquiry and the National Science Education Standards: A Guide for Teaching and Learning.* Washington, D.C.: National Academy Press, 2000.

American Association for the Advancement of Science. *The Atlas of Science Literacy.* Washington, D.C.: AAAS, 2001, 2007.

Arter, J. H., and Salman, J. R. *Assessing Higher Order Thinking Skills: A Consumers' Guide.* Bellingham, Wash.: Northwest Regional Education Laboratory, 1987.

Benson, M. *Beyond: Visions of the Interplanetary Probes.* New York: Harry N. Abrams, 2003.

Benson, M. "Celestial Sightings." *Smithsonian*, November 2003.

The Best of Edison Science Teaching Kit. Newark, N.J.: Charles Edison Foundation, n.d.

Blendinger, H., and others. *Win Win Discipline.* Phi Delta Kappa Fastback no. 387, 1998.

Bloom, B. *Taxonomy of Educational Objectives.* Boston: Allyn & Bacon, 1984. See also www.coun.uvic.ca/learn/program/handouts/bloom.html, last accessed August 12, 2007.

Bono. "This Generation's Moon Shot." Editorial. *Time*, November 7, 2005.

Bons, E. *Practical Entomology.* West Bend, Ind.: Fireside Books, 1992.

Borman, S. "Chemical Biology of the Cell." *Chemical and Engineering News*, December 11, 2006, pp. 34–35.

Borowec, A. "A Comparison of the Effectiveness of Two Methods of Reviewing Assigned Physics Problems on the Problem-Solving Performance of Non-Major Physics Students," Doctoral dissertation, Poley Library, Temple University, 1968.

Bracey, G. "The 15th Bracey Report on the Condition of Public Education." *Phi Delta Kappan*, October 2005.

Burke, J. *Connections* TV series. Washington, D.C.: Smithsonian Associates, 1979.

Business Higher Education Forum. "An American Imperative: Transforming the Recruitment, Retention and Renewal of Our Nation's Mathematics and Science Teaching Workforce," June 13, 2007. [www.bhef.com]; last accessed August 12, 2007.

Butler, S. M., and McMunn, N. D. *A Teacher's Guide to Classroom Assessment*. San Francisco: Jossey-Bass, 2006.

Dan's Manual of Mineralogy, 15th ed. Hoboken, N.J.: John Wiley and Sons, 1949.

Enabled/Disabled: Science Education for an Independent Future. Danbury, Conn.: American Association for the Advancement of Science, 1991.

Evans, J. *The History and Practice of Ancient Astronomy*. Oxford, U.K.: Oxford University Press, 1998.

"Getting All Revved Up." *American Scientist*, January-February 2007, pp. 24–25.

Gorbachev, M. title n.a. *Civilization*, September 1993, pp. 82–83.

Gore, A. *The Assault on Reason*. London: The Penguin Group, 2007.

Gough, N., and others. "Size, Mates and Fates." *Science*, December 1, 2006, p. 1409.

Grigg, Wendy S., and others, *The Nation's Report Card: Science* 2005, *Executive Summary*. National Assessment of Educational Progress, 2006. [http://nces.ed.gov/nationsreportcard]; last accessed August 12, 2007.

"Is It Time to Shoot for the Sun?" *Science*, July 22, 2005, pp. 548–551.

Jacobs, M. "Editorial: On the Nature of Discovery." *Chemical and Engineering News*, July 15, 2003.

Jones, V. F., and Jones, L. S. *Comprehensive Classroom Management*, 5th ed. Boston: Allyn and Bacon, 1998.

Kohn, A. "Abusing Research: The Study of Homework and Other Examples." *Phi Delta Kappan*, September 2006.

Langone, J. *How Things Work*. Washingon, D.C.: National Geographic Society, 1999.

Lewis, S. D., and Dubner, S. J. *Freakonomics*. New York: HarperCollins, 2003.

Margulis, L. "President's Message" column. *American Scientist*. November-December 2005.

McMunn, N. D., and Schenck, P. SERVE's Creating Effective Student Assessment Handbook for Participants, Bay District Schools Target Training. Unpublished training resource. (Cited in S. M. Butler and N. D. McMunn, *A Teacher's Guide to Classroom Assessment*. San Francisco: Jossey-Bass, 2006.)

Miner, D., and others. *Teaching Chemistry to Students with Disabilities, A Manual for High Schools, Colleges and Graduate Programs*. Washington, D.C.: American Chemical Society, 2001.

National Almanac Office of the U.S. Naval Observatory. *Physical Photometric Data Astronomical Almanac.* Washington, D.C.: U.S. Government Printing Office, 2005.

National Research Council. *Inquiry and the National Science Education Standards: A Guide for Teaching and Learning.* Washington, D.C.: National Academies Press, 2000.

National Research Council. *Science Medicine and Animals: A Circle of Discovery.* Washington, D.C.: National Academy Press, 2005.

National Research Council. *Taking Science to School: Learning and Teaching Science in Grades K–8.* Washington, D.C.: National Academies Press, 2007.

New Commission on the Skills of the American Workforce. *Executive Summary: Tough Choices or Tough Times.* City: National Center on Education and the Economy, 2006. [www.skillscommission.org/executive.htm]; last accessed September 17, 2007.

Phillips, Tony. "Saturday Morning Science." Science@NASA, February 2003. [www.science.nasa.gov/headlines/y2003/25feb_nosoap.htm]; last accessed August 12, 2007.

Rau, G. "How Small Is a Cell." *The Science Teacher,* October 4, 2004, pp. 38–41.

"Reading Between the Lines." *Smithsonian,* March 2007.

Saliba, G. "Greek Astronomy and the Medieval Arabic Tradition." *American Scientist,* July-August 2002.

Schmuckler, J., and Snyder, S. "Malachite." *Chemistry,* December 1975, 49(11), pp. 56–57.

Siegfried, T. "In Praise of Hard Questions." *Science,* July 1, 2005, pp. 76–77.

Sutman, F. X., and Guzman, A. *Improving Learning in Science and Basic Skills Among Diverse Student Populations.* Washington, D.C.: ERIC Clearinghouse for Science, Mathematics, and Environmental Education, 1995. [ERIC# SE 057-052].

Sutman, F. X., and others. "Hands On Science and Basic Skills Learning by Culturally and Academically Diverse Students: A Testament of the IALS." *Journal of Curriculum and Supervision,* Summer 1997, pp. 356–366.

Texley, J. "Safe Science Facilities." *The Science Teacher,* September 2005, pp. 39–42.

Wallace, C. "The Myth About Homework," *Time,* August 29, 2006.

"Water and Ice." *Science.* August 7, 2002.

"Water Works: Research Accelerates Advanced Water Treatment Technologies." *Chemical and Engineering News,* April 7, 2001.

Index

DATE DUE

Demco, Inc. 38-293